Ken's

Cruising Yacht

By

Ken Hellewell
www.kenhellewell.com

A Cevennes Productions Endeavor

Cevennes Productions

Edited by Sarah Cypher
www.threepennyeditor.com

Printed in U.S.A.

ISBN# 978-0-9727492-2-0

Acknowledgments

My wife Laurie gave me the precious time I needed to finish this book. I would never have finished it without her support.

It generally goes without saying that an editor improves a book but mine did so with a remarkably sensitive touch that wholly preserved my voice. Any mistakes are a result of my ignoring her suggestions. My stubbornness should not reflect poorly on her. I am also quite grateful for James Hancock's blunt and honest appraisal of an early draft. His comments greatly improved the tone and content.

Other books by Ken Hellewell:

*Ken's Comprehensive Cruising Guide
for the Kingdom of Tonga*

Ken's Torres Strait Passage Guide

Contents

Introduction i

Why Listen to Me? iii

My Philosophy 1

The Boat 5

The Rig 19

Sails 25

Ground Tackle 31

The Engine 43

Electrical System 49

Water System 57

The Galley 65

Electronics 73

Self-Steering 83

The Monitor 87

Yacht Tender 97

Provisioning 105

Navigation 109

Emergency Preparedness 113

Where In The World 119

Is It All Worth It? 123

Introduction

As I was preparing for my offshore adventure, I moved my C&C 38, Topaz from Seattle to Olympia. It did not take long after I docked Topaz at Westbay Marina for my new neighbors to learn that I was preparing to head offshore. For most sailors, it is constitutionally impossible to resist sharing an opinion on how things should be, and everyone had advice. Some was good, some bad, and some just perplexing.

Despite the fact that none of my neighbors had crossed an ocean or dropped the hook in a foreign anchorage, they all had something to say. The result was an ocean of freewheeling and contradictory advice. This dynamic is repeated every day in every marina around the world. A slew of books, magazine articles and Internet forums pile on even more information and suggestions. All this advice and conversation is fun and thought provoking, but it can be too confusing and contradictory for a beginning cruiser.

As I prepared for my cruising experience, I read all the books and listened to the opinions of many dock-bound "experts." It required a lot of sifting but I was able to find most of the answers I was looking for. When it comes to books, everything by Nigel Calder is a required addition to your shipboard library. Books by the Dashews and Beth Leonard are brilliant. These books contain just about everything you need to know before heading offshore in your own boat.

Unfortunately, none of the books does what I have attempted in this volume. None gives you the simple answers. They give you all the options, and all the pros and cons, and then let you decide. Unfortunately, for most of us, their approach is like handing us a West Marine catalog and saying, "Pick what you want, it will all work." Well, it won't all work.

It is not possible to just pick and choose from among all the options and end up with a reliable and effective result.

I take the outfitting of a boat system by system and tell you exactly what will work. I do not pretend that there are not other ways, maybe even better ways. What I suggest is that if you follow my advice you will have success. Your systems will be reliable. They will be safe and they will serve you well. Within the framework I lay out is plenty of room for individual tastes and desires. By using my advice as a foundation, you will save your cruising experience from the possible inconvenience and disaster of an outfitting mistake.

The suggestions in this book are mine alone. I expect many people, even you, to disagree with some of what I have written. That is expected. Nowhere in the world is a pair of sailors who agree on everything, because in truth, there is no single answer to any question regarding long-term cruising and ocean crossings. There is no single answer, but some things do work better than others, and some methods are more reliable. Here I offer the kind of advice I wish I had read before I purchased Topaz.

This book is not intended to be purely prescriptive. Nor is it exhaustive. I look at it as a printed version of what I would tell you if you walked up to me in the marina and asked for my advice. Within the framework of what I think a cruising yacht should be, all my advice is sound. If you agree with my philosophy, then you can trust that what I suggest will work for you.

If you are thinking about buying or outfitting a cruising yacht, this book was written for you. Consider it your personal conversation with someone who has already done it.

Why Listen to Me?

Sailing solo tests the sailor as well as the boat. During my solo circumnavigation I had no one to take the wheel, hold a wrench or hoist me up the mast. I was regularly called upon to reef the sails, raise the anchor, claw my way off a lee shore and enter reef passes by myself. I depended on the boat, her systems, and my ability to a degree unnecessary on crewed boats. In every way, sailing alone reveals the strengths and weaknesses of a boat and her systems. The experience taught me a lot about what I did right, what I did wrong, what works, and what doesn't. Over the years and sea-miles, I acquired knowledge and experience that will benefit anyone planning a cruising adventure.

I look at the planning and preparation of a yacht from a single hander's perspective. It stands to reason that if my methods work for a solo sailor, they will be even more effective when there are more hands available to share the responsibilities. This view gives me confidence that the advice I offer here will help you choose an effective route to your cruising dream.

A Note Regarding the Text

As you read the book, you will notice that I often refer to storms and possible disasters. This is not an attempt to be dramatic. Thinking about worst-case scenarios is critical to successful planning and preparation. If you, your yacht, or its systems are not prepared for the worst, then failure is assured. No long-term cruiser escapes nature's wrath.

Ken Hellewell

Photo Murrell Timmons

My Philosophy

My Philosophy

The advice in this book is predicated on the belief that you and I share similar views and goals of what cruising should be. This section defines my perspective. If you find yourself agreeing more often than disagreeing, then my advice will serve you well. If you think I am totally wrong, this book might not be for you.

Being Average Is Best

The spectrum of cruisers and their yachts is as wide as humanity itself. At one end are those who are a rickety boat and a can of beans away from absolute destitution. At the other end are owners who are whisked aboard by helicopter and who never allow a drop of seawater to sully their silken outfits. Between those extremes are the rest of us.

Our boat will be worth more than hundreds of dollars and less than millions. It will be big enough to host parties but not so big as to need paid crew or be limited to deep commercial harbors. We are looking to experience the wonders of the sea and different cultures around the world. We are not escaping the law or merely on vacation. We are not so far out of the mainstream that locals and other sailors exclude us from invitations. We are "cruisers" who want to experience everything the word is meant to convey.

We sail average-sized boats and live on an average-sized budget but have experiences that are everything but average. We also benefit by choosing boats and equipment that the majority of sailors have used and proven sound. No cruiser can ever be called an average person, but within the cruising community, being average really is the best place to be.

Cruising Is Not Camping

Human beings have an astounding capacity for adaptation. In fact, the ability to adapt to an ever-changing environment is crucial to a cruiser's happiness. Cruising is nothing if not a lifestyle of extremes. There is no separating the extreme highs from the extreme lows; they are conjoined twins. Fantastic sailing weather will eventually give way to storms capable of testing the toughest sailor's resolve. Wonderful people and places have their alter egos as well, and can drag down even the highest spirits. I have had days of unbelievable wonder filled with spectacular vistas and soul-warming camaraderie, only to return to my dinghy to find it loaded with garbage and smeared with shit. The cruising life contains more than enough drama. There's no point in adding to it by setting sail in an ill-prepared boat.

Your yacht will be your home. It will be more than just a method of transit and place to sleep. It will become your sanctuary. Whatever you need to meet your requirements for comfort and satisfaction must be carried with you. I part philosophies with anyone who thinks that cruising has to be one of living by candlelight, doling out fresh water by the spoonful, and eating a cuisine of re-hydrated peas. Happiness aboard can best be achieved by closely replicating your life ashore. Life aboard will never be exactly the same, but it can be close.

For cruising couples, open communication in this matter before leaving is crucial. Generally speaking, men can adapt to conditions far meaner than most women would prefer. If it is important for a partner to have a shower every day, incorporate it into your plans. Everyone is different. We all have particular requirements for our happiness. Do not assume that somehow the wonder of faraway lands and a life of adventure will supplant those needs, they won't. Deprived of our small luxuries, we will eventually tire of the cruising life. Once tired, the yoke will chafe and resentment will brew. Cruising is not camping, and what one can endure for a day, a week, or even a month will be unbearable when the journey stretches into years.

Maintenance Is a Job, Not an Adventure

There are some individuals for whom the task of varnishing a mile of teak is pleasure unto itself. I am not one of those people. If I had wanted to paint hulls, polish stainless, and varnish brightwork, I would have gotten a job in a boatyard. Keeping a cruising vessel's systems functioning requires plenty of effort. I believe cruising should be a life of exploration and new experiences, not a perpetual exercise in drudgery.

To that end, the boat should be as low maintenance as possible and its systems should be easy to use and dependable. The ocean and long distance sailing are brutal enough. There is no reason to make it worse by starting with a substandard setup. If you design and install your systems properly, using the right equipment, they should not fail. That, at least, is the goal. Good design is critical, and when it comes to hardware, "great customer support" is not the same as dependability.

The Boat

The Boat

Confidence Is Key

What kind of boat is best? No other subject attracts such a wide range of firmly held opinions. There is the full keel, heavy displacement camp, and they oppose the fin keel, light displacement people. You have your skeg rudder folks and the spade rudder disciples. Then, of course, there are the ketch vs. sloop vs. cutter crowds. Forget it all. Forget it until you meet the most important criteria of all: confidence.

Sailing the oceans of the world taught me that just about any yacht can make it. There are boats crossing oceans that I would not trust tied to a dock. This is not to say that seaworthiness is irrelevant. It isn't. A well-found boat is crucial. How many masts it has isn't. Your confidence in your yacht is what will make the endurance of a nasty storm possible. That confidence will free you from the fear such experiences can create and it will allow you to continue to point the bow seaward.

Whichever yacht you choose and whatever type she happens to be, make sure that you are absolutely confident in her. This holds true for every aspect, hull, rig, and systems. Don't let others talk you into things that leave niggling doubts in the back of your mind. Those doubts will grow into bowel churning anxiety when the storm hits.

Imagine you are alone in the middle of the ocean, as you may someday be. Out of nowhere, a 40-knot wind slams into the boat, bringing with it 20-foot waves that are churning and breaking. The foam is flying and the bow pulpit is barely visible through the spray. You have no idea how long it will last or how much worse it will get. The above is possible. If you circumnavigate, it is likely. When it does, will you be worried about the hull splitting or the rig going over the side? Will you wonder if the self-steering will fail and force you behind the wheel? Can your sail plan endure the howling gale for days? Imagine the rest of your crew is disabled by sickness or injury. The goal is to do your best to ensure that when it does, you can rest comfortably below deck, confident that you will survive to see one of the greatest sights on earth: a post-storm sunrise.

You most likely already have some strong preferences. Don't let my words influence you into abandoning your core beliefs any more than you would the dock bound "experts" who have never put to sea. The truth is that selecting a yacht is as emotional as it is logical. Sailors are partial to certain types of boats, and their biases will affect their choices. If you are a lover of traditional ketches with acres of brightwork, there are not enough logical arguments in the world to make you buy a rocket shaped sloop without a speck of wood in sight. Luckily, suitable cruisers exist in every shape, size, and configuration. Just make sure that whatever you choose, you trust her absolutely.

The Short Answer

If I was going to purchase another yacht to cruise in, I would buy something very close to Topaz. I would probably get something a little bigger, but she would be fiberglass or metal with a fin keel and a spade rudder. I would want her to be light displacement but strong and very maneuverable. I would want a draft in the neighborhood of 6' with a non-encapsulated keel. Her rig would be a sloop or cutter with a staysail. I would love for her to have oversized rod rigging and a relatively short boom. The headsail and staysail would be fitted with roller furling. And now that you know what I think, let me tell you why.

Hull Material

Fiberglass and metal are your best options. Fiberglass boats outnumber all other types of construction. For this reason alone, fiberglass is a likely choice. When one considers its low maintenance, excellent track record, and range of choices in shape, size, and style, fiberglass truly stands out as one of the best materials for the average cruiser.

Metal boats can be tempting and not without advantages. Chief among them is that you worry less about getting holed. If you plan to head into iceberg territory, metal is the only option. Metal boats can also be constructed to all but eliminate leaks. But they do have disadvantages. A steel boat will need to be completely gone over and most likely stripped to bare metal, have its welds and plates inspected, and be re-primed and painted. Moderately sized steel boats also tend to be heavier and thus slower.

Aluminum is a cruiser's dream metal and I confess to some lust for it. Unfortunately, there are very few aluminum yachts for sale. Unless you are going to custom build in aluminum or absolutely must have steel, then the odds are you will end up with fiberglass.

Do not consider wood or ferro-cement. Wood will consume your life with its maintenance needs. This is especially true in tropical waters where worms and rot will attack with a vengeance. Ferro is heavy, fragile, and rife with unknowns regarding its construction. There is no good reason to buy concrete or wood.

This reasoning holds true for custom boats as well. Whether it is a custom fiberglass, ferro, or cold molded wood, custom one-off boats come with mystery as well as uniqueness. You never know what might have happened that late Friday night when the epoxy was kicking off a bit too fast and a cold beer was calling. Along this same line, if you are contemplating building your own, try to resist the temptation. It is a rare and extraordinary person who is capable of completing this monumental feat.

If the concern of landing a fiberglass boat on a reef and losing her makes metal seem like the only option, consider the following: In most of the places where yacht destroying groundings are likely to occur, the means to haul a boat back to sea will be unavailable. A steel hull is much more likely to remain intact but that is a small consolation when your yacht is permanently lodged on a reef.

Fiberglass is an amazing material, but it also has its own shortcomings. Delamination and osmotic blisters top the list. Catastrophic delamination (when sections of the hull peel away) is extremely rare among well-made production yachts. Small-scale layer separation is common. Cored hulls are more susceptible to delamination because the connection between the core and the fiberglass is a potential weak point. Pound for pound, however, a cored hull is stronger than its non-cored counterparts. Topaz had a cored hull, and I was grateful not only for its strength but for its insulating properties; the layer of balsa kept the interior more comfortable in hot and cold climates.

A good survey can identify areas where delamination is occurring. You can check yourself by tapping on the hull with a hard object. Any areas with voids or delamination will sound hollow or dull. Also, pay close attention to the areas around hull penetrations. Some delamination can be easily repaired, others not. Avoid any boat with large-scale delamination, because it is a sign of a poorly laid hull as well as a repair nightmare. A yacht with serious delamination issues is not cheap at any price.

Blisters are another matter. Until a yacht has spent time in the tropics, it is impossible to know if she will develop blisters. I know many cruisers who left the States in a yacht with a seemingly perfect hull, and after a short season in Mexico, their "perfect" hull developed hundreds of blisters. Some brands and vintages are better than others, but there are no guarantees. The best way to avoid blisters is to buy a yacht that has already spent some time cruising in the tropics. The other way is to buy one that has already had an epoxy barrier coat applied or apply one before you leave.

Size Does Matter

Given a choice between a 27-foot example of marine fastidiousness and a strong but grubby 40-footer, I will choose the 40-footer. When the sea gets rough, would you rather be on a log or a cork? A bigger boat is faster, more comfortable, and better able to carry all the stores and amenities that make long term cruising a pleasure. Every couple and individual needs their own space. Remember, we are talking months and years. For the average single hander or cruising family, a yacht between 35 and 50 feet is the best choice. Any smaller and it will be too crowded and less comfortable underway. Any bigger it becomes too difficult to handle, and your visits to smaller and shallower anchorages will be restricted.

Bucking Tradition

If books and dockside "experts" have convinced you that the only safe way to cruise is to strap yourself into the heaviest-displacement, fullest keeled, and smallest rig possible, then there is little I can do to change your mind. A look at any anchorage around the world will show that this view is no longer the conventional wisdom. It used to be. Fin keeled, light-displacement cruisers used to be rare, and now they are everywhere.

This is certainly due in part to advancements in design and technology and the resulting explosion in the production of fin and modified-fin keeled boats. It is also due to the learned realization that these modern yachts make great cruisers and they have many advantages over their traditional brethren. Disagree? Consider the following.

The numbers of cruising boats lost while crossing an ocean is so small that they do not even register as a percentage. Regardless of one's fear of half-sunken containers, whales, and ships on autopilot, the true danger to a cruising yacht is land, land being any piece of the earth that can possibly come into contact with a yacht's hull. With very few exceptions, these pointy pieces of earth are located in or near the harbors you will choose to visit. Therefore, maneuverability is one of the most important safety features a yacht hull possesses. Is the assumed greater oceangoing stability of a traditional yacht worth a loss of maneuverability? I say no. It is also not worth the loss of speed.

Speed is not only a luxury. It is also a safety feature. My first passage to the Marquesas from Mexico took 28 days. My second only took 19. Those extra nine days at sea were nine extra days where something could have gone wrong. They were nine extra days exposed to Mother Nature, container ships, and fate. The first passage was aboard a slow, heavy displacement ketch and the second was aboard Topaz. The ability to make decent speed in light airs is what made the difference.

I am not saying you should avoid full keels or heavier displacement. The best cruiser, however, has a balance of desired characteristics. I would no more want to put to sea in a jittery rocket than I would an over ballasted slug. Your yacht should be just as safe short tacking through coral heads as it is surfing down a wave.

The Keel

A maneuverable cruising yacht suggests a fin or modified fin/full keel. For so many reasons, I would choose maneuverability over a traditional full keel. Whatever configuration you choose, make sure that you are comfortable with and confident in your yacht's handling. Imagine sailing through various hazards in a contrary current and a strong crosswind. It will happen.

Whether you choose fin or full, you will also have to decide if it should be encapsulated. My first boat had a fiberglass encapsulated keel. I always felt more secure knowing that even if the keel bolts failed, the fiberglass would prevent the lead from dropping to the seabed and the boat turning turtle. When I purchased Topaz I was less than thrilled that her keel was not encapsulated. I remember staring at the six bolts and wondering just how strong they were after a quarter century and a circumnavigation. Not until I saw what happens to an encapsulated keel when it hits a reef did I learn to appreciate the superiority of a bare keel.

Fiberglass cannot withstand the crushing force of lead smashing against coral or stone. If the top of the keel is not sealed, a hole in the encapsulation is the same as a hole in the hull. Even if the encapsulation is properly executed (meaning that water cannot pass into the boat's interior), repairing the damage requires an extended stay in a boatyard. It takes a long time to remove enough saltwater to make the repair a successful endeavor. Most places you are likely to visit do not have the equipment required for hauling out anything bigger than a rowboat.

While writing my cruising guides, I used Topaz to explore potential new anchorages, and I cannot remember how many times I bumped into underwater obstructions. The soft lead of her keel bore the scars of these many collisions. When I was finally able to haul her in South Africa, I found coral growing where a few pieces got embedded during a particularly nasty grounding in Tonga. A little hammering and some epoxy filler, and within minutes the keel was as good as new.

For pleasure sailing, I don't think it makes much of a difference. But if you head offshore, I suggest a strongly fastened keel with nothing but bottom paint covering it. If you still opt for an encapsulated keel, do whatever it takes to ensure that a keel breach won't sink your boat.

The Rudder

No part of the boat endures more stress, strain, and relentless demands than the rudder. If any part of your boat's rudder even *looks* weak, you best address it. It, like the keel, hangs low and is at risk for collision. It should be strong enough to endure a moderate blow. It also needs to be robust enough to endure 100 times the work and wear of the average pleasure yacht. If you find a racer/cruiser that has some age but never really sailed offshore and its rudder is already feeling loose or sloppy, then it is probably not strong enough to endure long-term cruising. If I had to choose between being dismasted and losing the rudder, I would kiss that mast goodbye.

Tip: Many of the modern and more efficient hulls have flatter, less tapered sterns. They are great for sailing speed but some have a tendency to slap explosively in bumpy anchorages. I have seen sailors go so far as to strap pads to the hull to quiet the surprisingly loud and sleep depriving noise. I would consider this tendency to be a deal killer when choosing a boat.

The Deck

If you plan on spending any time in the tropics, your deck color needs to be as white as possible. The darker your deck is, the hotter it will get. Even an ever-so-slightly darker, cream-colored deck will get much hotter than a white one. This will not only necessitate shoes when walking on it, it will also significantly raise the below-deck temperature. It gets hot enough with a white deck. There is no sense making it worse by choosing a colored deck.

The same applies to teak decks. Teak looks great and its traction when wet is remarkable. Barring that, teak decks are nothing but a bad idea. They get very hot in warm climates, most are prone to leaks, and all add a huge amount of weight where it is least needed—well above the water line. If you absolutely must have teak, accept the fact that you will endure hot cabins, a scorching deck, and eventual leaks. The choice is yours but I wouldn't have them.

Before you fall in love with your dream boat, consider its deck layout. The two most important aspects of a great cruiser's deck are storage space and clear walkways fore and aft. Space to carry a ready-to-deploy dinghy will make every port of call both safer and more enjoyable. Clear walkways are a comfort and safety issue. Take notice of any obstacles such as standing rigging and control lines. There should be an unobstructed path that allows you to run between the bow and stern with the boat heeled over as well as at anchor. You will have plenty of occasions to do both, and many of those dashes will be performed at the very worst times in the very worst conditions.

When it comes to deck storage, I believe that your spare dinghy, life raft, and related items are all that should be stored topside. Although traditional, strapping jerry jugs full of water and fuel to the lifelines is the silliest of practices. Topside is the last place you want more weight. The sun and heat are enemies of stored water and fuel. Furthermore, lifelines are not made to bear the brunt of a crashing wave hitting a wall of jugs. There are better and more convenient ways of storing water and fuel below decks.

For the items you do need to store, adding strategically placed pad-eyes will make storage easier and more secure. You don't want a web of lines running around the deck. Like all deck hardware, make sure the pad-eyes are through bolted. A blue water cruiser is no place for screwed-in hardware. While you are at it, inspect your lifeline stanchions. It seems hard to believe, but there are boats out there with lifelines held to the deck with screws. It is important that the lifelines are robust, but even the best lifelines should be a last resort for the sailor heading over the side.

Jacklines

When moving about the boat while underway, you are wise to stay closer to the center of the boat. Not only is the center safer, it is also where you want to be as you are most likely heading forward to do something with the sails. This is where I also depart from tradition. In almost every example of jackline installation, the jacklines are run next to the lifelines on both sides of the boat. I believe this is patently stupid. If your harness is long enough to reach from the lifeline to the mast, then it is long enough to allow you to be dragged through the sea.

The jacklines should be as close to centerline as possible. That way, with a short tether, you can never be forced over the side. This is absolutely logical, but for some unknown reason almost everyone strings their jacklines around the outer edge of the deck.

The very best jackline setup would be a tautly strung cable from the center of the cockpit to the mast and then to the center of the bow. If you use a double-ended tether that allows you to hook around the mast, you can have just one jackline running right down the center of the boat. This method is better, safer, easier to use, and install.

Cockpit Dodger

Topaz came with a custom hard dodger. I took advantage of its protection more times than I can count. I cannot imagine putting to sea without some kind of protection from the wind, rain and crashing waves. Having a dodger not only offers protection from the elements, it is the perfect place to mount a solar panel or two.

If you can manage it, I suggest you have a hard dodger made and installed. It will be better able to withstand crashing waves than a canvas version. If canvas is your only option, it is vastly better than nothing.

When fitting and choosing a dodger, make sure that it offers good visibility. Also ensure that the dodger is tightly sealed to the deck. Any gap and jets of water will shoot into the cockpit when a wave forces its way between the dodger and the deck.

Interior Configuration

Unless you perform a complete interior remodel, the interior configuration will be whatever your chosen boat happens to come with. Even so, don't shortchange yourself. You are purchasing a home. The boat's interior is where you will be living, sleeping, and entertaining. It does not need to be fancy, but it does need to be comfortable and secure. The interior deserves at least as much attention as the sail plan.

Sleeping Arrangement

When choosing a yacht, most people run down their checklist of "most important" things and likely miss one of the biggest ones, proper sleeping arrangements. At anchor, just about anywhere in the boat is a fine place to spend the night. When underway, that is decidedly not the case. Berths that are comfortable at the dock can become unbearable when sailing. The forepeak turns into a trampoline and sleeping on the uphill side of a heeled-over boat is uncomfortable and potentially dangerous. In bad weather, four habitable cabins can quickly be whittled down to one.

I am astounded by the new so-called cruising yachts that have berths on just one side of the boat. Sure, with lee cloths or boards, one can sleep anywhere, but I would not want to. In the event of a serious knockdown a lee cloth or board may not prevent a person from flying out of bed. Make sure that all the crew have a comfortable berth regardless of the tack. Also make sure that you have plenty of berths aft of the keel to accommodate everyone.

Head Location

Head location is not a deal killer, but it is worth consideration. The vast majority of all sailboats have their head shoehorned in between the forepeak and the salon. This works, but it is not ideal. In rough weather, relieving oneself can test a contortionist.

I never gave the matter much thought until I saw a yacht with its spacious head and integrated shower located right next to the companionway. It was brilliance! This location not only makes it easier to use the restroom when underway, it is perfect as a wet locker. Whether coming in to rinse off sand and saltwater or to peel off your soaked foulies, you will not have to traipse the length of the boat to do so. Give bonus points to any yacht with a head near the companion way.

Lighting & Fans

Install reading lights and fans in every location where you and your crew will sit and sleep. The new LED lights are amazing power savers and multi-speed fans preferred. Keeping the house lights on to read or work will quickly deplete your batteries and more often than not a fan will be required to keep you comfortable. They also help keep mosquitoes off your face. (A better way to avoid mosquitoes is to anchor a quarter-mile or more from shore. Not to be too mercenary but if you anchor further out than other cruisers the mossies will get them first.)

The Rig

The Rig

Unless you are a committed ketch or sloop fan, the rig you get will come with your yacht of choice. In other words, people tend to choose the yachts they love and trust, and that includes the rig. No reasonable person buys a ketch and turns it into a sloop or vice versa. If you are a ketch person, nothing I can tell you will change your mind. That is fine. Any rig will work. While there is no reason to get into a ketch vs. cutter debate, I would like to review a few of the advantages and disadvantages of each.

The Ketch

One of the biggest advantages to a ketch is the spare spar. Having a second spar is comforting, especially when you imagine a rig failure that results in a lost mast. I always figured I could use the spinnaker pole as a jury rig, but it is a lot easier to use a mizzen. The second advantage is balance. A mizzen simplifies the task of setting the sails because it can be used like the tail on a kite to balance the main and headsail. On a reach, a ketch can often be set to steer herself without an autopilot or wind vane.

The disadvantages of a ketch start with the added topside weight and clutter. Additionally, the need to carry another set of sails is no small burden on a moderately sized yacht. Ketches are less efficient, tend to be slower, and cannot point nearly as well as a sloop. While some ketches do all of the above better than some sloops, generally speaking, sloops are simply better sailers. Just look to the racing community for proof. Those who say speed is not important have not spent enough time counting the miles, days, and weeks of a passage. As for pointing, if a gentleman never goes to weather, then gentlemen never go cruising.

The Sloop

If you reverse the advantages and disadvantages of the ketch, you just about have it covered. Sloops are simpler, speedier, and point better. With fewer sails, sail management can be much easier. Reefing in a blow is tough enough without adding another sail to the mix. I made passages during which I could expect one to ten squalls every night. On these passages I would have stopped using a mizzen altogether.

The Bottom Line

The fact that thousands of people cruise with all kinds of rigs proves that no single type is mandatory. As a single hander I would not want to bother with a mizzen; the advantages are not worth it. Most of the world agrees. The ketch and the heavy displacement yacht have given way to the lighter displacement sloop. I say embrace progress and join the crowd.

Other Rigs

I will not cover other rig types because they make up such a tiny percentage of cruising yachts. I am not a rigging expert and cannot speak to every advantage and disadvantage of every kind of rig. The owners of each type can certainly offer a thousand reasons why theirs is superior. Perhaps they are right. Knowing how a sailor's loyalty for his or her yacht can infect the most critically capable mind, I prefer to follow the example of sailing and racing professionals worldwide. The day I see the America's Cup and Around Alone racers adopt the gaff rig is the day I begin to consider it the sloop's superior.

Rig Configuration

The best way to explain my position on this subject is to say that any sailor who follows the conventional routes around the globe will spend a lot of time sailing dead downwind. They will also get caught in at least one ugly storm a year. These truths make swept back spreaders and a giant boom undesirable. Swept back spreaders make it difficult to sail dead downwind and a long boom can be a nightmare in heavy weather.

In the open ocean, variable sea and wind conditions make sailing downwind a trying experience. The boat bobs and yaws and the mainsail does everything it can to flop, flog, and backwind. Even with the main flat against the spreaders, some angle off the wind is necessary to keep it steady. If you have swept back spreaders, this angle will need to be much greater. The added spar support offered by swept back spreaders is not enough of a benefit for me to forgo the ability to sail more directly downwind.

I expect most sailors who endured a storm with a long boom wished for a shorter one. It takes little imagination to understand why this is so. Even Topaz's short 12' boom dipped into the sea on numerous occasions. Imagine a boom five or ten feet longer. This same boom will need to be controlled during a gybe.

I would have hated dealing with eighteen feet of aluminum (or worse, cedar) hurtling across the deck. Additionally, it is much easier to manage a smaller footed sail when reefing, which you will have many, many opportunities to enjoy.

Wire vs. Rod

Is any subject regarding yachts uncontroversial? It is certainly not the rod vs. wire debate. This is another case in which either will work just fine. Wire is, without question, the most popular choice for world cruisers. In the racing community, rod rules. The reasons are clear: Rod is lighter, stronger and stiffer. For the average cruiser, the cost of switching to rod might be unjustifiable. But if you are planning on re-rigging your yacht, it might make sense. Before you decide against rod, let me debunk some myths.

There are really only three strikes against rod rigging. The first is cost. The second is the difficulty in predicting rod failure. The third is the inability to repair rod or carry spare sections. Except for these issues, rod is superior in every way. For me, one of the biggest advantages to rod was how gentle it is on the sails. Downwind passages regularly called on me to lay the main against the stays. I never had a chafe problem. The rod also stays cleaner and never corrodes. Then, of course, there is the cool factor.

When it comes to cost, the comparisons are often unfair. The initial install of rod costs significantly more than wire. But on the other hand, rod lasts much longer—so much so that I would submit that the cost per year is actually less than wire. The rod on Topaz has already lasted nearly 20 years. If rod is oversized and rigged to eliminate flexing and work hardening, it will last a very long time.

When rod breaks, there is often no warning. This does not mean, however, that you cannot see signs of impending failure. Rod can now be installed with sleeves that break to indicate excessive flexing and signal the need for replacement. Even without the sleeves, close inspection can reveal undue pitting or points where the rod is work hardening. It is not always possible to tell if a rod is weakened, but neither is it always possible to see wire failing. More often that not, the interior, longitudinal strands inside of a wire go first. I have had several wire failures, and I never saw them coming.

The repair issue does have some merit, but not much. In the unlikely event of a rod failure, the broken section can easily be replaced with wire. By carrying a spare length of wire and appropriate end fittings, this argument against rod evaporates. In the middle of the Indian Ocean, one of the lowers broke when Topaz gybed with a poled out headsail. It was a vicious gybe, and a mid-ocean jury rig ensued. Had I been better prepared I would have been able to make a cable with some Norseman fittings and installed a wire replacement on the spot. I finished my circumnavigation with the wire replacement I installed in Darwin. The bottom line is that with some preparation, overcoming a rod failure is no more difficult than a wire one.

Conventional wisdom suggests that cruising vessels should have oversized rigging. Rod lets you do just that without becoming top-heavy. You also reap the benefits of rod rigging's low-stretch, corrosion-free, and sail-friendly characteristics.

Sails

Sails

It makes no sense to start an extended cruising adventure with worn-out sails. You should have a set of sails that can withstand the rigors of several years of sailing with two serious storms per year thrown in. If you cannot afford new sails, then make sure the ones you have are newly repaired, re-cut for proper shape and that the material has a lot of life left in it. I have seen cruisers try to get by with worn sails, and in port they sat on the foredeck, re-stitching seams, and adding patches. Having to repair sails is bad enough. Losing the use of a sail partway through a passage is terrible. Your sails are not going to fail when the going is nice or when an underway repair might actually be entertaining. They will fail when the last thing you want to do is crawl out on the foredeck with a flashlight, a ball of thread, and a needle.

The Mainsail

A fully battened mainsail is the only way to go. I am not a racer and was never too concerned with the optimum shape and settings that a fully battened main is designed to provide. For me, the beauty of full battens is the control they offer in all conditions. They are especially helpful when the winds become lighter. When a non- or partially-battened main flogs, a fully battened main will stand stable and proud. This not only reduces wear on the sail; it reduces wear on one's nerves. The battens also keep the sail extended and ready to pick up occasional puffs of wind. With the addition of lazy-jacks, the battens also make reefing and stowing much easier. If you have a high aspect ratio main as I suggest, the newer graphite impregnated sail slides and nylon connectors eliminate the need for expensive and heavy bat-car systems.

Reef Points

I barely knew anything when I ordered my headsail and main from North Sails. I had read all the books and even crossed an ocean, but I still made the huge mistake of ordering my main with just two reef points. Fortunately, North's cruising sails are extremely well-made and mine endured regular over-deployment. Make sure you have a third reef and make sure that it is extremely deep. When fully reefed, your mainsail should rise no higher than ten feet above the boom. If you have to use your main in a blow, you won't want to deploy more than that.

The Headsail

Your roller furling headsail should be moderately sized. The best way to minimize the negative effects on sail shape caused by a flying a partially furled sail is to fly it unfurled as much as possible. My headsail was about a 110. If you have a relatively light displacement yacht, I would not suggest one much bigger. There were times when it would have been nice to have more sail area, but the vast majority of the time, the 110 was plenty.

You want your headsail to be made of material heavy enough to withstand a wide range of conditions. There will be times when the weather turns and you will need to fly a postage-stamp-sized corner of the sail. Nature does not always give warning. If your plan is to change between a heavy weather sail and a whisper thin one for lights airs, the time will come when nature catches you with the wrong sail up. The ensuing trapeze act will negate the couple of extra miles you might have gained with your musical sails strategy. Fly a single, universal headsail and use a gennaker if you want light air speed.

The Whisker or Spinnaker Pole

I know they are not the same thing. But one day, as I was sailing along with my adjustable whisker pole fully extended, the combination of heeling too far and an oddball wave dipped the pole in the water. That was the last time I used it. An "L" shaped pole is hard to use and even harder to stow. For the next four years, I was forced to use my spinnaker pole.

What followed was one of those unplanned bits of good fortune. My spinnaker pole was exactly the same length as the distance from the mast to the head stay, meaning I could leave the spinnaker pole attached throughout the complete range of headsail deployment. When a squall roared through, the ability to quickly furl the headsail without going forward to adjust or remove the spinnaker pole was priceless.

Racing purists might cringe at my sail configurations, but with a judicious use of the spinnaker pole and the sheet, I maintained total control of the headsail. In really light airs I would crank the sheet tight, and the force on the spinnaker pole would pull the headsail out and into a nearly flat surface. I lost some sail shape, but I also got rid of the flogging.

In heavy wind I would let out a few feet of sail. Again, I would keep the sheet tight, causing the pole to pull the sail away from the head stay. In rough stormy waters the added sail control kept the sail in position during the wild gyrations of the bow as it plowed through the waves. It also allowed me to sleep better knowing the headsail was under control. I was always willing to sacrifice half a knot for silence and sail longevity. If you want your sails and your sanity to survive the long haul, you will be too.

The Staysail

Most cruising yachts do not have staysails. This is clear proof that they are not required. This is not proof, however, that they are not desirable. For those who want speed, in the right conditions, a staysail can add a welcome boost. For me, the staysail was a piece of safety equipment. In heavy weather, a staysail shines. It is smaller, closer to the deck and easier to manage than any full-sized headsail.

Because my staysail was of the hank on variety, I tended not to use it as much as I would have had it been roller furled. The times I needed it most were the very same times I did not want to leave the cockpit. Deploying a hank on sail in a blow is not my idea of fun. If I were to do it again, I would make sure that my yacht had a heavy-duty roller furled staysail.

Even though I did not regularly use my staysail, I was grateful for the extra stays. When I left Cape Town I suffered a frightening knockdown. The boom and part of the mainsail dipped in the water. I was fully reefed with both of the staysail running backs employed and cranked tight. I am certain this added support helped prevent a dismasting. If nothing else, the thought of another set of stays adds peace of mind.

Tip: A close hauled staysail will help funnel wind into the headsail. This is especially helpful in light airs.

Lazy Jacks

As seen in this diagram, lazy jacks work best when attached to the spreaders and the boom. Mounting the upper pulley about a foot from the mast will prevent the lines from slapping against it. Running the lines to cleats on the boom helps with this as well. It also allows one to tack and gybe with the lazy jacks raised. The cascading loop arrangement ensures that all of the legs of the lazy jacks are equally taut. This also makes it possible the tuck the the lazy jacks behind the boom cleat and adjust the tension to keep them there.

Getting the lengths and geometry just right will take some measurement or trial and error. I suggest making each leg extra long. Then you can hang the set, adjust everything properly and then just cut off the extra where it attaches to the boom.

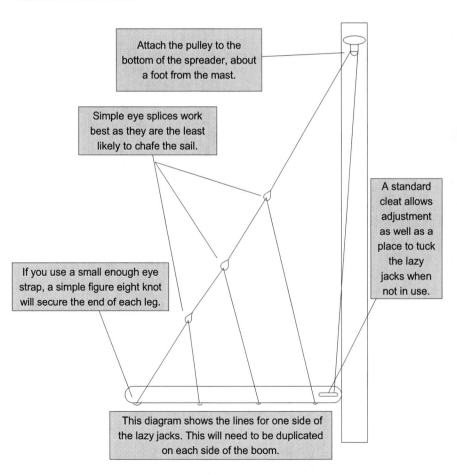

Attach the pulley to the bottom of the spreader, about a foot from the mast.

Simple eye splices work best as they are the least likely to chafe the sail.

A standard cleat allows adjustment as well as a place to tuck the lazy jacks when not in use.

If you use a small enough eye strap, a simple figure eight knot will secure the end of each leg.

This diagram shows the lines for one side of the lazy jacks. This will need to be duplicated on each side of the boom.

Ground Tackle

Ground Tackle

Bigger Is Better

I have never seen a cruising yacht with too many anchors or with chain that was too big or too long. Three hundred and sixty-five nights a year you will go to bed with your confidence in your ground tackle the admission price for a good night's sleep. I have known many cruisers who stand anchor watches when the winds are stronger than a breeze. This is no way to live. Ninety percent of the time, a ball of chain resting on the bottom is enough to keep you and your boat safe. The other ten percent of the time, avoiding disaster will depend on the choices you made when selecting your ground tackle.

Do not size your anchor and chain based upon manufacturer's recommendations. If you do, your anchoring system will be sorely undersized. The suggested sizes for anchors, chain, and windlasses are all made with limitations on conditions. The suggestions seem to be based upon an assumption that the boater can quickly up anchor and jump back into the slip. This is rarely an option for cruisers. As with everything aboard, your ground tackle needs to be sized to handle the worst possible conditions.

Chain

> 300' of 3/8" (minimum) *new* chain in the bow
> 50'–100' of 3/8" chain for stern/emergency hook

The conventional wisdom is that world cruisers need 300' of chain. While it is possible to get away with less, after a couple of years of daily use, you will want to end-for-end it. We have already established that you are sailing on a yacht 35' or greater in length, therefore, 3/8" is the smallest chain you will want aboard. You can get just as much strength from a smaller "high test" chain, but you want the added weight. Extra weight affects sailing performance, but so will the massive, reef-induced hole in your hull. The weight of the chain is what keeps it lying on the bottom when the wind picks up. You will spend the majority of all your time at anchor. The extra weight is worth the security.

Make sure your primary chain is new or nearly new. I left with new chain, and by the time I returned home, it was absolutely worn out. Living on the hook is hard on your ground tackle, and it makes no sense to start out with anything less than perfect. You and your boat depend on it.

World cruising is not like lake sailing. Only chain can withstand the rigors of living on the hook. Some suggest that it is possible to reduce the weight in the bow by using a rode and chain combination, their theory being that you can use the rode for the section that never touches the bottom. Their theory is flawed. No matter how vigilant you are, the chain and rode connection is a potential weak link, and there is no guarantee against chafe. I have seen a 1" rope chafe all the way through in less than a day. The margin for error is too small. Buy peace of mind by sticking with chain.

Tip #1: Always try to anchor in water no deeper than you can snorkel. With a little practice, a fit person can dive 30' to 50'. If your chain or anchor gets fouled, it is nice to know that you can dive down and likely resolve the problem. By anchoring in shallower water, you will also use less chain. That leads to Tip #2.

Tip #2: By using a piece of heavy duty PVC pipe and with a little modification, I was able to fashion a secondary storage area at the head of the forepeak berth. This allowed me to store half of the chain a dozen feet aft of the chain locker. By anchoring in shallower water I was able to use a 5:1 scope minimum while keeping half my chain in perfect condition. In an emergency, the chain would self-feed forward.

Anchors

Primary bow anchor: 45 lb. (minimum) plow or spade type—C.Q.R., SPADE, Delta, etc.

Second anchor: Fortress FX-37 or larger

Third anchor: Bruce, plow or spade type, 35 lb. or larger

Do not leave the dock with fewer than three anchors. There are occasions when you might need all three. In Aitutaki, the lagoon is very shallow and swing room is limited. I had to use three anchors to keep Topaz perfectly positioned over the only location slightly deeper than her keel. Even if you never need three at once, there are without question times when you will need a bow and a stern anchor. Along the way you just might find a way to lose an anchor; people do. If you only carry two and you lose one, you will be handicapped. It is not easy to replace anchors outside the world's population centers.

Like the rest of your anchoring system, your anchors need to be oversized; they need to be *way* oversized. I suggest buying anchors two sizes larger than manufacturers' recommendations. The added size and strength will be the difference that prevents your yacht from dragging. The terror of sitting aboard your yacht as it drags toward a lee shore as the bow bucks and crashes into surging waves will immediately banish any concerns about a few more pounds on the bow.

The vast majority of cruisers settles on a plow or spade type anchor as their primary hook. This is for good reason. Although getting a plow anchor to set properly can be a challenge, it is still the best choice for combination bottoms. Fluke type anchors have a holding strength that is unbeatable, but they are absolutely limited to sand and mud. Most of the world's anchorages are strewn with rock, coral, debris, or all three, making a fluke type anchor less than useless. Many people swear by Bruce anchors, but there is no getting past the fact that they do and will become fouled. Once a Bruce has picked up a chunk of coral or rubbish, they become a nearly useless ball. They set very fast and this makes them an excellent choice for a backup anchor or a stern hook, but I would never use one for my primary hook.

I spent an unforgettable night in Suva thanks to a violent rainstorm that scoured the harbor. Several times I went out in my dinghy to assist yachts with fouled and dragging anchors. Three boats collided with each other in what seemed like some kind of twisted comedy routine. Interestingly, all the boats that had problems were using Bruce anchors. The anchors either failed to hold in Suva's muddy bottom or became fouled by tires, corrugated roofing, and other garbage.

Having said that, cruisers more experienced than I swear by the Bruce. They have used the anchor for years with very few foulings. People use and love what they trust. If you happen to love them, though, keep in mind the Bruce's potential to foul.

Windlasses

Electric windlass: 1300 lb. min. with power-up/down

Don't even think of going to sea without some kind of windlass. It may be hard to believe, but I have seen yachts without one. Watching the crew trying to retrieve an anchor from coral would be humorous were it not so pathetic. More than that, it is dangerous.

Choose an electric windlass. Honest cruisers with a manual windlass will admit to leaving the boat hanging tenuously at least once when they should have re-anchored. On occasion I have re-anchored as many as five times to get a good set. Doing this with a manual windlass stretches the capability of the strongest crew.

Most of the windlasses sold in marine chandleries have no place aboard a cruising yacht. They are aimed at the casual boater and won't last a year of typical world cruising. They are simply not made for abuse. Even many of the ones with high power ratings are just geared-down versions of less powerful models. If the windlass instructions require you to use the boat's engine to take the load off the chain before retrieval, the windlass is too small. If the windlass manufacturer's ratings tell you the windlass is sized for your yacht, it is too small. Are you getting the picture?

You not only want lifting power, you want a windlass that can take the shock loads of a pitching bow and a chain caught up tight in a coral head. Your windlass needs to be strong and powerful enough to shrug off any kind of abuse you can possibly inflict. You want an industrial-strength beast. It will get you out of trouble and it will last much longer than a marginally constructed one. I am not saying it needs to be the size of a guesthouse. I am saying it needs to be robust. There are very strong and powerful windlasses made that are also quite compact.

Now that you have decided to install a mechanical behemoth on your foredeck, make sure the deck can handle it. Install a thick backing plate below the deck. This plate should be as wide as possible. The goal is to transfer the load to a very wide area. It is especially beneficial to transfer the load to the hull deck joint. The last thing you want is for the windlass to pull itself out of the deck.

Install a remote switch in the cockpit. There really is no reason that anchoring should require more than one person. I have anchored hundreds of times and always by myself. Having a switch in the cockpit just makes the process easier. It is also a backup for when your foredeck control stops working (as it will) because of the constant exposure to seawater. Instead of foredeck switches, use a wired handheld control. The ability to move around the deck while anchoring comes in handy, especially when deploying and retrieving the snubber. Besides, who wants to drill two big holes in the foredeck?

Tip #1: Do not install a separate "windlass battery" forward to save on conductor size. The battery won't be big enough and it totally messes up your charging system. Just don't do it!

Tip #2: Install huge conductors between your battery bank and the windlass; the bigger the better. Smaller conductors cause resistance, which causes heat, which causes more resistance and an ensuing snowball of resistance, heat, and current draw that will end in failure. Once your conductors become overheated they will begin to corrode and fail.

Tip #3: The cost of installing your windlass will cost as much as the windlass itself. The wiring, switches, and labor are expensive but ultimately worth it.

Tip #4: When using your windlass, always try to have your engine running and charging. This will allow your alternator to take the load off of the batteries. Batteries do not like heavy loads. They, too, will heat up and their life will be drastically shortened.

Snubber

Always install a snubber on your anchor chain. Not even an oversized windlass and bow roller will survive the shock of a chain repeatedly pulled up short. A snubber adds flexible resistance to the boat's motion. It will dampen, quiet, and protect the boat.

I used the largest Line Master rubber snubber with ¾" braided line and a chain hook. The chain hook allows a quick and secure chain connection. Even though the chain hook had no positive latching mechanism, it never once came off of the chain. I strongly suggest you avoid any snubber–chain connection that cannot be undone in a couple of seconds.

The rubber snubber worked in the very worst conditions and lasted my entire circumnavigation. But there is a caveat. When I first tried this combination I wrapped the line around the snubber half a dozen times, just as people do when using it at a dock. This will not work. The first time a storm hit, the snubber was ripped in half with a spectacularly explosive "BOOM!" I learned that two wraps around the snubber allow plenty of cushion before the rope reaches its limit. This prevents the snubber from overextension.

The constant dunking of the snubber line and perpetual exposure to the sun causes it to deteriorate much faster than the other lines on your boat. Inspect it regularly and replace it if it looks at all worn, because braided rope can rot from the inside out. I learned this the hard way. An unexpected storm in Madagascar put me on a lee shore exposed to a very long fetch, at which point the snubber line failed and the chain made a good attempt at tearing the windlass out of the deck. The one spare I did not have was a chain hook. The next morning I made dozens of dives in the murky, still-rough water to find the hook and snubber. With my nose dredging the bottom, I finally managed to spot them. You might want to bring some spares.

Trouble-Free Anchoring

Some couples and crews have developed effective hand signals and routines that eliminate the yelling, confusion and frustration that is routinely seen in anchorages. Others, clearly, have not. I always dropped the hook by myself, even when I had guests aboard. This was not an unwillingness to delegate; it's just that two pairs of hands is unnecessary. If anchoring causes you any distress, give my method a try. It is effective and even enjoyable.

As you head toward your intended anchoring spot, aim for it with the wind on the nose. Lower the anchor off of the roller. As the boat slowly drifts toward the point where you want the anchor to rest, let out about the same amount of chain as the water is deep. This will make pinpoint precision dead simple. It won't matter if you misjudge a bit and let out too much chain. The anchor won't set until you have some scope laid out.

By the time you get to the desired spot, the boat should have just about come to a stop. You now want to lower the chain as the boat reverses course. If there is enough wind, it will push you back. Even so, just pop the transmission into reverse idle and start lowering the chain. Well before you have laid out your desired scope (I suggest 5:1 at all times, space permitting), the anchor and chain will be dictating the boat's speed. After you have laid out all the chain that you want, rev the engine up to its max operating RPM. This will help ensure the anchor is set. A successful anchor deployment is one that firmly sets the anchor and leaves the bow of the boat pointing into the prevailing wind. The chain should be laid across the seabed without any piles of chain.

The entire process happens slow enough to allow one person to walk back and forth between the bow and cockpit. If you have a windlass control in the cockpit, you should not have to make any trips forward.

This assumes that you have your anchoring system properly sorted. Your windlass should power both up and down. Your anchor and chain should freely deploy and be retrievable without manual assistance. Granted, I pushed Topaz's anchor off of the roller manually, but I did this easily on the way to the anchoring spots.

If you have a bowsprit with a bobstay, take special care in the implementation of your anchoring system. There will be times when a crosswind or current will cause the anchor chain to drape across the bobstay. In trying conditions, the chain can actually become locked against the bobstay, making it impossible to raise the hook. I have seen it happen. The best solution I have seen is a piece of PVC pipe slid over the bobstay.

Windlass

Over time a yacht's ground tackle system endures more abuse than any other piece of equipment. A properly functioning windlass *can* prevent disaster. If at all possible make sure every part is new, well over-sized, and installed properly. Even the best system can fail so make sure your windlass has manual override capability.

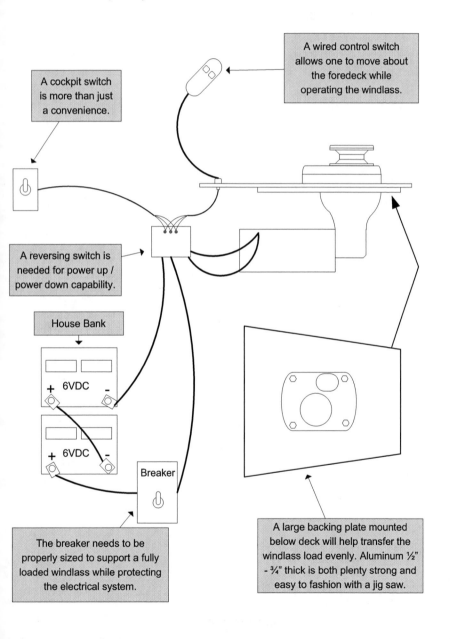

A wired control switch allows one to move about the foredeck while operating the windlass.

A cockpit switch is more than just a convenience.

A reversing switch is needed for power up / power down capability.

House Bank

+ 6VDC -

+ 6VDC -

Breaker

The breaker needs to be properly sized to support a fully loaded windlass while protecting the electrical system.

A large backing plate mounted below deck will help transfer the windlass load evenly. Aluminum ½" - ¾" thick is both plenty strong and easy to fashion with a jig saw.

Anchored in Agua Verde, Mexico

The Engine

The Engine

You absolutely must have an engine, and it needs to be reliable. People can and do head off to sea without one. Some do so for financial reasons and others because they want to experience a form of sailing "purity." This is my pet peeve. I have no problem with people who decide to sail engineless as long as they never, ever, ask other cruisers for a tow. Unfortunately, this almost never happens. The most famous engineless sailors write their books and conveniently leave out the number of times they have been towed. If you sail without an engine and rely on others to tow you, then you are not sailing engineless; you are simply using someone else's engine. This behavior is highly hypocritical and puts both parties at risk.

Cruisers do not get to choose the weather. When they arrive at a port, they have to deal with whatever nature brings. Several ports around the world are nearly impossible to enter during bad weather. If an engineless sailor arrives at one of these ports, he or she will either need to wait out the bad weather or, if conditions allow, ask for help. Virtually every cruiser will leap to the assistance of a fellow sailor. Sometimes asking for help cannot be avoided, but if you have decided that you want to be a "purist" by sailing without an engine, you have absolutely no right to ask another sailor to risk boat, dream, and possibly life for your sake.

Beyond the safety concerns, not having an engine changes everything. It will limit where you can go, affect your passage-making, and it will drastically reduce your creature comforts. For most yachts, the engine is also the generator and few things are more important than a reliable supply of electricity.

Unless you have gobs of money to spend, you will end up with whatever brand and model of engine that comes with your yacht of choice. This is not a horrible thing unless the engine happens to run on gas. If so, you absolutely must replace it. A gas engine has no place aboard a cruising yacht. It is dangerous, and fuel supply and quality are limited.

If your dream yacht has a gas engine, look on the bright side—you will have the opportunity to install a brand new Yanmar. There are plenty of good engines out there and just about all marine diesels will serve you well. Other cruisers might disagree, but this is my book and my opinion, and for my money there is no better choice than a Yanmar. Other brands have better distribution chains, which makes getting spare parts easier, but the beauty of a Yanmar is that you will likely not need to find parts.

Whatever kind of engine your yacht has, verify that it is in tip-top shape before you leave. Do some research and find out if your model has particular weaknesses or tendencies. The best way to do this is to talk to a reputable mechanic that specializes in your engine type. They will know if your engine blows head gaskets every 1000 hours or if the injector pump is finicky. Carry spares for any part your engine is likely to need. At a minimum, I suggest carrying a spare fuel pump, water pump, and a complete set of raw water pump parts including a rebuild kit and impellers. Also take a close look at the starter, and consider carrying a spare. The smartest move would be to install a new starter and keep the old one as a backup.

My Yanmar 3GM30-F had a handle that was supposed to allow me to start it manually. Near as I can tell this was either an engineer's fantasy or an intentionally cruel practical joke. My few attempts over the years resulted only in skinned knuckles and a sense of utter futility. If it was ever possible to start the engine by hand, it must have been some ordeal.

Tip #1: If at all possible, arrange your pulley system so that your water pump and alternator are on separate belts. The added belt tension and vibration of the alternator is the number one reason for premature failure of water pumps.

Tip #2: Try to make sure you end up with a freshwater-cooled engine. If you are heading to sea with a used raw-water-cooled engine, you are looking at the beginning of the end.

Tip #3: Make sure your exhaust system is ready for the long haul. Heat and saltwater is a brutal combination. Exhaust systems rot from the inside out, so dig a little deeper and make sure your aqualift and hoses are truly fit.

Tip #4: Carry plenty of spare oil and filters, and use them. Consider using multi-viscosity oil. In the tropics the single viscosity oil recommended by my engine manual resulted in unstable and sometimes low oil pressures. A change to high quality multi-viscosity oil improved everything.

Tip #5: Many yachts have horrible engine access. Do your best to ensure that you have adequate access to all the parts of the engine that require periodic maintenance. Fast access to the belts and raw water pump is crucial.

Motoring through the Panama Canal

Fuel System

By using your auxiliary tanks to fill your main day tank it is easier to keep track of your remaining fuel and usage. This configuration also keeps your fuel supply isolated in the event of contamination. If your yacht does not have auxiliary tanks it is quite simple to install Nauta flexible tanks. Make sure the fill and vent tubes are are on the high side and the outlet tubes on the low side of the tanks.

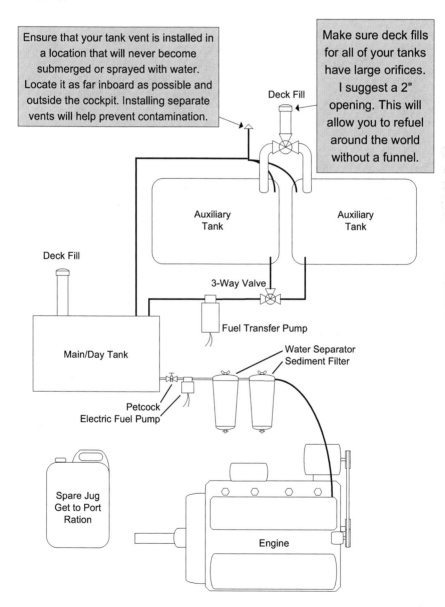

Ensure that your tank vent is installed in a location that will never become submerged or sprayed with water. Locate it as far inboard as possible and outside the cockpit. Installing separate vents will help prevent contamination.

Make sure deck fills for all of your tanks have large orifices. I suggest a 2" opening. This will allow you to refuel around the world without a funnel.

Deck Fill

Auxiliary Tank

Auxiliary Tank

3-Way Valve

Deck Fill

Fuel Transfer Pump

Main/Day Tank

Water Separator
Sediment Filter

Petcock
Electric Fuel Pump

Spare Jug
Get to Port
Ration

Engine

Electrical System

Electrical System

Electricity changed the world, and there are few things that affect day-to-day living quite as much. The same is true aboard your yacht. I have seen yachts with virtually no electrical system, and conditions aboard were more primitive than the average cruiser wants to endure. We tend to think of sailboats as wind powered vehicles, yet a cruising yacht is powered as much by electricity as it is by diesel or wind. Having a reliable supply of electricity is important for too many reasons to list here in full, but a few of the biggies come to mind. Starting the engine is pretty important. So are navigation lights, VHF radios and even the ubiquitous GPS. Do not shortchange your electrical system. Make sure it is robust, properly installed and not overly complicated.

The Batteries

Do yourself a favor and install a large battery bank. Your minimum amp hour capacity should be about 1000Ah. If you want to use 12VDC refrigeration on a regular basis, make your bank even bigger. Think of your battery bank just like you would a fuel tank. Size equals range, and in the case of a battery bank, size also affects efficiency.

Notice that I used the word *bank*, not banks. Just about every boat ever made comes with two battery banks. I suppose the idea is that there will always be one bank that is fully charged when the other goes flat. Usually, these banks are just two separated batteries that serve the purpose of two starting batteries. While I completely agree with the idea of having a spare starting battery, extending the concept into two, full-fledged house banks is not good. In fact, the entire concept is rife with shortcomings and contradictions.

What might work at a dock will not work for long-term cruising. To begin with, it is crucial that all the batteries in your bank start out as new and identical. During charging, the entire bank takes on the characteristics of the weakest battery. If you mix three new batteries with one that is on its last legs, the bank will soon act like four batteries on their last legs. It is just how they work.

The biggest reason one large bank is better than two smaller banks is efficiency. It is all about time and amp hours. When charging batteries, the closer they get to full charge, the fewer amps they can accept. The larger the bank, the more time your alternator will have to cram in more amps because it takes longer to get a larger bank closer to fully charged. This explanation is simplistic, but it is the truth.

Having just one bank also eliminates the complication of battery combiners, solenoids and other methods used to try and charge two banks. It also allows you to permanently wire your alternator directly to the bank which will drastically reduce any chance of blowing the diodes in the alternator. Having one bank is cheaper, easier, and more efficient. It is just, plain, better.

Battery Type

I had plenty of money when I outfitted Topaz. Enough, at least, that I could consider installing any kind of battery I wanted. I spent endless hours researching types and brands and found myself lusting after AGM and the Rolls Surrette. I love technology, and there was no way a standard lead acid battery could compete with the sex appeal of the latest in AGM or the moniker of the world's most renowned luxury car. Not even the relatively new gel cells of the day could turn my head. Topaz disagreed.

Her battery compartment is short and funny-shaped, so only a certain number of certain-sized batteries would fit. I was forced to start with the basics and figure out how I could squeeze the most amp hours into Topaz's battery compartment. Size and shape trumped technology. By resorting to 6VDC deep cycle batteries I was able to stuff many more amp hours into the compartment than I could have with the Rolls or AGM batteries. It all came down to battery shape and size. The reported efficiencies and superiority of the AGM and Rolls batteries could not overcome the raw volume of amp hours I was able to install using the pedestrian (and much, much cheaper) lead acid batteries.

I may have started my journey disappointed, but I finished it grateful. Five years later I sailed into San Diego with the same set of batteries aboard. They were tired and due for replacement, but they served me well and endured some remarkable abuse. No matter how you calculate cost, standard lead acid batteries are cheaper per amp hour. Replacements are also much easier to find. Try finding an AGM or Rolls battery in Tonga. Even gel cells are hard to come by. True, the more advanced batteries require less maintenance and are more tolerant, but this does not make them worth three times the cost. Save your money for more important things.

It is written just about everywhere that the full operating range of marine batteries is 10.5VDC to upwards of 13VDC. The theory is that by allowing them to discharge all the way down to 10.5VDC you will have access to a greater percentage of their capacity. This is true, but it ignores the life-cycle cost of discharging below 12VDC.

All batteries have a given number of life cycles. This is essentially the number of times they can be fully discharged before they die. Every time the batteries drop below 12VDC one of these life cycles is consumed. You can calculate that your batteries should last for a couple of years, but this calculation probably ignores the loss in efficiency that comes with every lost life cycle.

There are other reasons for a larger bank. By never letting your batteries drop below 12VDC, no life cycles are lost, so their full efficiency is retained, and they will last for years. Neither will you have cause to fret about having batteries too discharged to start the engine. This practice also provides a better power source for today's electronic equipment. Most marine electronics are designed to work with voltages as low as 10.5VDC but others are not.

Alternator(s)

How big should your alternator be? This is a complicated question. Topaz's battery bank had a capacity of approximately 800Ah. I installed a 115A Balmar marine alternator to charge the house bank and a 50A automotive alternator to charge an independent starting battery. This seemed about right.

If you follow my suggestion and never let your battery bank drop below 12VDC, your alternator will only be called on to deliver full power for a relatively short period of time. I submit that for a bank in the 700–1000Ah range, a 50A alternator would be just fine.

Exceptions to this are house loads. My windlass under load drew approximately 100A and an inverter running a water heater or microwave was about the same. The ability of the alternator to carry the bulk of this load will make it much easier on your batteries. They do not like heavy loads or quick discharging. Don't feel like you need a 200A alternator—because unless you have huge loads, you don't.

I was grateful for my dual alternator setup. In the diagram at the end of this chapter, I show a single alternator setup where the starting battery alternator has been replaced with a solar panel. Either way is good, and both cost about the same to implement. The second alternator is great to have as a spare, but installation on some engines can be tricky.

Whatever design you choose, make sure your primary alternator has a top-notch regulator, such as those provided by Balmar. You want the ability to customize your charging to suit your battery type and your lifestyle. You also want the ability to equalize your bank occasionally. This will keep your batteries healthy and their capacity at maximum.

Alternative Energy

There are so many options when it comes to alternative charging. Within each group of wind generators, solar panels, and towing generators exist dozens of choices. I think you can quickly reduce the confusion by opting to forgo anything except solar. Towing generators only help during passages, and in the scheme of things, you won't really make that many. As for wind generators, as much as I adore the idea, I have grown to hate them. If you have ever moored next to or anchored downwind of a yacht with an Air Marine aboard, you know why. I have changed anchorages to get away from the irritating screech.

It took me a couple of years before I fully accepted the truth that periodic running of the engine is the best method of topping up the batteries. I know a wind generator seems like a great thing, but it isn't. Even if you learn to love the constant sound, your neighbors won't. There is nothing wrong with running the engine. For my money, I would put the thousand dollars you will spend on a wind generator in the diesel budget.

I love solar and believe having at least one panel is mandatory. There may come a time when it is your only source of badly needed electricity. Depending on your budget and daily power demands, it is possible to get all your electricity from the beautifully silent panels. Most likely, however, they will only supplement your requirements. That is just fine. Again, there is nothing wrong with running the engine.

Tip #1: If your engine is moderately sized, you will want a switch in the exciter circuit to allow you to stop the charging cycle. A large capacity alternator fully loaded saps the engine of a surprising amount of power. There will be time when you will want all the power your engine has to give.

Tip #2: Diesel engines do not like to be operated unloaded. A diesel running at idle will start to develop carbon deposits that will shorten its life. Therefore it is not a good idea to sit at anchor with the alternator dribbling 10–15A into the batteries. Try to do your charging while underway, or you can put the transmission into reverse while at anchor. Your engine will thank you.

Electrical System Charging & Storage

This diagram assumes you are using 6V batteries in series wired pairs . The key is to ensure that your alternator is wired directly to the battery bank . This prevents the leading cause of alternator failure which is opening the connection between the alternator and the bank . A starting battery connected to a small solar panel will keep it ready to use if your main bank ever becomes too discharged to start the engine . This should never happen if you adhere to the #1 rule of battery maintenance : Never let the battery voltage drop below 12.0VDC.

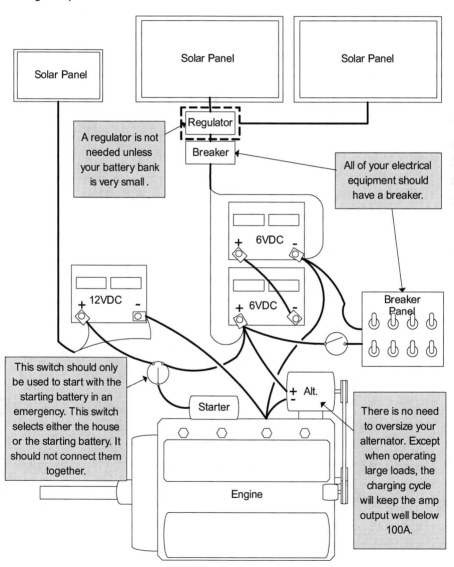

Water System

Your water system affects both life safety and luxury. In this context, life safety means enough water to survive, and luxury means regular showers—even regular hot showers. When designing your water system, it is crucial that you plan for the worst-case scenario. This means enough water to provide everyone onboard with life-sustaining rations for not only the longest passage but for a disastrous event.

Imagine a mid-ocean knockdown that dismasts the boat and incapacitates the engine. Sufficient water will allow you to limp into port under a jury rig. It would be a shame to use your EPIRB and abandon your yacht and your dream because you ran out of water. Even with an EPIRB, rescue cannot be guaranteed, and water is the only thing you absolutely must have to survive for any length of time.

Beyond life safety concerns, your water system should be reliable, redundant, and easy to use and maintain. While it is unnecessary to have a fully pressurized system with hot water on demand, it sure is nice. Having to hand or foot pump every ounce of water you use will contribute to conservation, but it is also tiring. It is one of those things that can make cruising like camping—and therefore something to avoid. A properly designed water system will give you plenty of water and take you as far away from drudgery as you desire.

Capacity

At a bare minimum, you must have a safe and secure supply of at least ten gallons per person. This emergency ration cannot be an imagined part of single tank because a tank may become contaminated or spring a leak. You need at least two tanks aboard, and at least one of them must be big enough to contain your emergency ration. It is OK to alternate your emergency supply source as long as you *know* that you always have the minimum amount in an uncontaminated and accessible location.

There are three ways to guarantee a sufficient supply of water. The first and least appealing is extreme rationing. This method effectively eliminates the luxury aspect of your water system. Another is having large capacity water storage, but a yacht can carry only so much water before its sailing performance is affected. The last is having a watermaker aboard. Watermakers are expensive, require maintenance, and are subject to failure.

Do not let other books persuade you that catching rainwater is a reliable way to get fresh water. There are only a few anchorages in the world where it rains regularly enough to catch water as needed. Trying to catch water during a passage is especially difficult. Sure, there will be times when nature's spigot will run freely, and you should be prepared to take advantage of a convenient rainstorm, but do not even think of including rain in your water supply calculations.

Topaz came with two 30-gallon tanks. They were the factory installed poly tanks that most yachts have under the settee seats. I did not feel sixty gallons was enough, so I boosted my virtual capacity with a PUR 40-E watermaker. This saved me from the dreaded "camping" environment that hauling water jugs, measuring-cup baths, and rationing create. Like a big battery bank and extra fuel tanks, a watermaker adds range, which equates to safety and freedom. I know that a watermaker is expensive and it also uses its fair share of power. When calculated by the gallon, however, the power usage is minimal. When the total cost is divided by the number of years you plan to cruise, it is an inexpensive way to buy ease, freedom, and safety.

The PUR 40-E could have easily supported another person. If you are planning on cruising with four or more people, you may find it a little on the small side. It is rated to make about 40 gallons every 24 hours, but who wants to listen to a watermaker run 24/7? At 1.5 gallons per hour, I tended to run the watermaker two to three hours per day, some days more, some days less. I liked the idea of allowing myself five gallons per day. A five-gallon day allowed plenty of water for drinking and cooking as well as a darn nice shower.

To the experienced cruiser, five gallons is a lot of water. The neophyte will find it a challenge to adjust to this level of consumption. Unless you have lived aboard, your first shower will probably empty a tank and shock you into reality. A residential water-saver showerhead expels 2.5 gallons per minute. When a ten-minute shower blows through 25 gallons, try to imagine surviving a 30-day passage with just the water in your tanks. This is another reason to consider a watermaker. A functioning watermaker is a virtual bottomless tank.

I counted on my watermaker, but I was always prepared for a failure. I made sure that one of my tanks was always full and used the watermaker to replenish my regular usage. Had the watermaker failed I would have immediately placed myself on rations. One must always know how much good water they have at any given time.

This is why it is crucial that you have redundant storage. I heard many stories of cruisers who had an entire tank compromised by either a leak or seawater that found its way down the tank vent. For this reason, I moved one of my tank's vents and fill port inside the boat. This complicates filling, but it virtually eliminates the possibility of contamination.

As in the fuel system, using flexible tanks can expand your water supply. They can be installed in voids that are not readily accessible, and can be used for emergency stores or day tanks. One of the great things about flexible tanks is that they do not require a vent; they simply collapse and expand as they are emptied and filled. If your yacht's tanks are the standard poly tanks, there is probably a lot of unused space in the compartment where they are located. A custom-made flexible tank can greatly increase your water capacity by taking advantage of all the available space. I would suggest sticking with a trusted manufacturer like Nauta. Don't take a chance on cheap imitations.

As an added level of safety, I suggest storing a supply of bottled water aboard. I kept 24 individual bottles in my abandon ship buckets. I loosely calculated that I could get by using two bottles per day. Canned vegetables and soups are also valid sources of emergency fluid.

Pumps

I highly recommend a pressurized water system. It costs very little and makes every day a little bit nicer. Manually pumping a glass of water is not a big deal, but having to pump all the water for a shower will greatly diminish your pleasure. Shurflo pumps are, by far, your best option. They are self-priming, can run dry without damage, and come with a built-in pressure switch. Either the 2.8 or 3.8gpm models will work well. I suggest also adding an accumulator/pressure tank. These are tanks with a pressurized bladder inside that "store" water pressure, which reduces pump cycling and smoothes the water flow. Install the pump in a location where its operation can be heard, which will help you monitor your usage as well as let you know if you have a leak or if a tank runs dry.

At least one manual pump is mandatory. If you lose power or your electric pump fails, the manual pump will let you get to your water. On that note, I suggest ensuring that you can get water from the tanks if all your pumps fail. For easily accessible tanks, the clean-out ports offer such access. If your tanks are not so accessible, using an air pump to pressurize the tank will force the water out of the tank and down the supply lines. Plug your vents first or you will pump a long time with no results.

I installed a second Shurflo for my gray water system, which also served as a possible backup for the pressure system pump. Neither died or gave me any problem despite one running dry for months when I left the boat for a return visit home. Another reason to have an electric water pump aboard is that they come in handy as a replacement for a failed raw water pump for your engine. I made a mid-ocean rendezvous with some friends whose raw water pump died in the treacherous Mozambique Channel. We plumbed the Shurflo into their engine cooling system, which worked great and made me feel pretty smart for having a pair of pumps aboard Topaz. Why not enjoy both a cheap insurance policy and a pressurized water system by installing a Shurflo aboard your yacht?

Water Quality

If all your water comes from a watermaker, it will be perfectly pure and clean. Rainwater is also sweet and sediment free as long as your catchments are not contaminated. When filling from an onshore supply, quality is not always certain. As it is likely that you will get water from all three sources, a sediment filter is a must. It will protect both you and your pumps from particles of sand, dirt, and vegetation.

Rather than a basic filter I strongly suggest one that also contains activated charcoal. The activated charcoal will eliminate that nasty taste that almost all boat water seems to have. They last up to six months, so you do not need to carry many of them.

Water Heater

A water heater is not necessary and many cruisers spend their entire trip using solar showers or a teakettle to make hot water for showers and dishes. You would not live this way at home, so why do it on the boat? By installing a water heater with a heat exchanger you will have hot water every time you run your engine as well as anytime you are plugged into shore power. If you want hot water available at all times, you will need to install a more sophisticated hydronic heating system. In my entire circumnavigation I had no need for cabin heat beyond what my paraffin lantern provided. As such, it is my belief that installing a sophisticated hydronic heating system is unnecessary, but I am not opposed to them. If you have one, you will use it, and the ready hot water is nice.

If you make it to Cocos Keeling you will have the opportunity to add to this cruisers' shrine. It was strangely touching to see the sing left by Lee and Mindy of New World. I met them long before I planned to go cruising aboard Topaz. That is how it is in the cruising life. Friends are met in one part of the world and then found again in another. It happens with a remarkable regularity. This far flung camaraderie is perhaps the most difficult to lose when your cruising adventure ends. It know it was for me.

The Galley

The Galley

This is where "cruising is not camping" really comes home. Do not saddle yourself with some half-thought-out compromises. Great food and the ability to prepare it daily are not only one of life's greatest gifts, they are critical to on-board happiness and health. The cruising lifestyle will probably be the most social environment you will ever experience. Food and drink are often the center of the merriment, and you will want to participate. You will be invited to many get-togethers and you may regularly be a host. On passages, cooking and eating are the days' milestones; they provide activity, entertainment, and nourishment. Your galley needs to be as usable, if smaller, as the one in your home.

Layout

Unless you are going to custom build or completely remodel your boat, the layout of the galley is a get-what-you-get proposition. Most are laid out fairly well, while others leave experienced cruisers scratching their heads. Because safety trumps all else, the galley needs to be arranged so that the stove is gimbaled and the chefs can position themselves securely while cooking. Wearing a harness is not enough. You need a place to wedge your feet, your bum and anything else you can possibly wedge. All of the above is further aided if the galley is close to the centerline. This is the most stable place on a boat.

If the galley aboard your chosen vessel is open or spacious, you will need a heavy-duty harness with attachment points that are just as strong. Both will need to withstand the full force of your body's weight in motion. If you can break them by lunging, the sea surely will.

The Stove

Gas stoves are the units of choice for the best chefs, and it should be for you as well. You can get by with two burners—heck, you can get by with one, but why? Even a simple meal of pasta and foccacia requires two burners and an oven. Make sure your stove has at least three and an oven. Of course, the stove needs to be gimbaled. While underway, and even in a rolly anchorage, it needs to be able to move freely to keep the pans in place.

Gas stoves can be deadly but propane is the only real choice. It is available everywhere you will sail, burns clean, and is easy to use. Other, safer alternatives are not readily available. With care and respect a propane stove can be safe and effective.

> *Oven Tip: Buy a pizza stone and store it inside the oven over the lower burner. Yacht stoves are notorious for uneven heating. The pizza stone will deflect the direct heat of the burner and improve the even distribution of heat. Your baking will be greatly helped by this addition.*

Propane Storage

Just like all the other items that involve quantities (fuel, batteries, and water), the more propane the better. I carried two 20-pound aluminum tanks mounted under my cockpit seat, and found this to be the perfect amount. I filled my tanks less often, which appealed to my natural laziness, and also had the freedom to spend months away from civilization. When one of the tank valves froze up, the remaining tank was big enough to keep me going.

Some yachts come with built-in propane storage compartments, but most don't. You need to find a place that is secure, ventilates freely, and is somewhat protected from seawater. I have seen propane tanks mounted on the foredeck, next to the mast and on stern rails. These are terrible places for many obvious reasons. Wherever you choose to mount yours, make sure that any leaks will vent the propane off the boat and not into any interior cavities. Propane is heavier than air, and given a chance, it will pool in a low spot and create a virtual bomb.

I used a dual tank regulator that allowed me to switch tanks on the fly. It was nice but unnecessary. By having large tanks, I only needed to switch them a few times a year. Just as easily I could have used two valves routed into one regulator. An even simpler and barely more difficult option is to move one hose between the tanks as needed.

I started out using an electric solenoid switched from the galley to control the propane supply to the stove. The unit came with a propane "sniffer" that set off an alarm in the event of a leak. My sniffer constantly went off without cause, so I removed it from the system before I even left the dock. This is not recommended, but I was unable to prevent the false alarms. As for the switch, it was a great idea. The only difficulty was keeping it working. As far as I know, a waterproof version of the solenoid does not exist, but their purpose as a safety device requires them to be mounted outside the boat.

This puts them into the same elements that the tanks endure. Mine, and many of my friends' units, failed.

When I installed my system, I used one continuous hose that ran from outside the boat to a valve located on the stove. Installation guidelines require that all lines inside the boat be hard piping such as copper tube. In my opinion, *and this is just my opinion and not an instruction*, I felt much safer having a flexible hose running through my boat. I feel that the flexibility of hose is much more resistant to damage when the boat is in motion. If you opt for the suggested hard tubing, make sure there are no joints that can fail. Using bendable copper, you should be able to have the complete run done with one continuous length. I would consider any soldered joints as weaknesses and potential failure points.

The Sink

Like many yachts, mine came with a shallow, single-reservoir sink. This is impractical for daily use. The sink is not only a place to wash dishes; it is a repository for the day's catch and a place to toss any number of wet and dirty items. If you can, install a double-basin model. Make sure it is as deep as it can be without it being below the waterline. I loved the depth of my new sink, but the basin closest to the hull would end up below the waterline when the boat heeled over. On passages, it would have seawater in it for days—a real pain. The closer to the centerline your sink is, the less likely this is to happen.

Kitchen Equipment

There is no reason to outfit your galley much differently than you do your kitchen at home. Bring your good pots and pans, your stainless cutlery and good knives. Stowed properly, everyday items are plenty rugged to endure life aboard a boat. If you decide to install an inverter, you may as well make it big enough to operate your kitchen accessories. Bring your blender and your food processor and even your coffee grinder. Some people swear by their pressure cookers. I did not own one before I went cruising and I did not take one with me; I don't see the need. I had a huge inverter, so I was able to use my microwave. Since you already own the things you use, if you have the room, bring them along. If you find that any of your appliances do not fit into your cruising lifestyle, you can get rid of them later.

Plastic plates are ridiculous. I did buy polycarbonate glasses and found them to be perfectly fine and truly worth the cost. This is the only concession I made to "break-proofing" my galley. It is the only one I see worth making. Bring the plates you are using now, your favorite coffee cups, and all the other things that make dining pleasant. Treat your galley, and the rest of your boat, as much like home as possible. It will be your home, and the fewer compromises you make the happier you will be.

Tupperware

There is no substitute. Before I left, my girlfriend became a Tupperware dealer. We took the starter pack and added an army of the stackable storage containers. I stored every kind of food as well as some hardware in them. They are stable, hold their airtight seals, and last forever. I cannot say enough good things about these absolutely essential containers.

Storage Tip #1: The blue 3-M masking tape used for painting makes excellent labels. They stay in place, are easily removed and never get gummy like other tapes.

Storage Tip #2: You can never have too many Ziploc bags in too many sizes. Avoid the cheap imitations.

Refrigeration

In my opinion, this is the single most difficult subject to cover. I would like to offer the best solution, but when it comes to refrigeration, I am afraid there isn't one. The decision to add refrigeration exposes you to an infinite number of choices and decisions. Not only will you need to decide what kind of refrigeration system to install, you will have to design your entire electrical system around your future refrigeration usage. No other item aboard uses as much power as a refrigerator. Even if you install an engine-driven compressor/holding plate system, you will need to adjust your charging system and schedule.

The simple fact is that without refrigeration, one can get by most of the time with a couple of solar panels. In the powerful Baja sun I was able to go weeks without having to run the engine. The solar panels were jamming 60–100Ah into the batteries every single day. On the hook, the only power I usually needed was for reading lights, the watermaker every other day, my stereo and computer. I had surplus power. Turning on a refrigerator changes everything.

All considered, if your refrigeration requirements are modest and you are happy with simple cooling and some occasional splurging, a 12V system like an Adler Barbour is perfect. These systems are simple and reliable, and I liked mine very much. If you install a large battery bank as I suggest, running the engine every couple days will keep up with it. I have heard positive things about the Technautics Cool Blue system, and I would likely choose it over and Adler Barbour if I were in the market.

If you decide that refrigeration is a must, do not skimp on the refrigerator box. Whatever box came with your boat, it is most likely inadequate. Your refrigerator box and its door need to be extremely well insulated and leak-proof. A custom box made with vacuum panels will save you hours of charging and cooling.

After a good meal

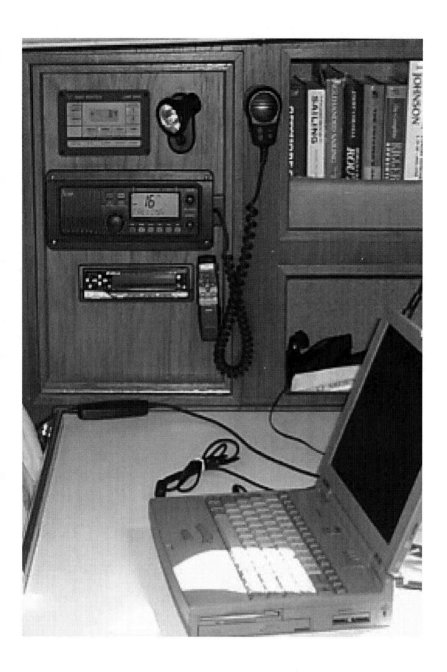

Electronics

Electronics

It is still possible to sail the world with little or no electronic equipment. Just because it is possible does not mean it is recommended. There are not many of us who would sail without GPS, depth sounders, and radio communications. Heck, I would not do it without a decent stereo. As a writer, at least one computer is required equipment. In just about every way, electronic equipment makes cruising safer, easier, and more enjoyable. I would go so far as to say that certain items are absolutely required. I would include the following on that list.

GPS

There is absolutely no reason why any cruiser, pleasure sailor, or even far ranging hiker should head out without a GPS. I carried three aboard, just in case. Anyone who talks down the usefulness of this world-changing product is a fool. I sailed without a life raft. I would never go offshore without at least one of these electronic marvels. The number of tools and options built into the better models offer a huge array of options that go far beyond just telling you where you are. Paired up with a computer and a radar display, sailing will seem more like the Enterprise than the Endeavor. Without a doubt, you will find a GPS to be one of the most used pieces of equipment aboard your yacht.

Garmin is the clear leader in this area and I can attest to the quality of their products. Sailors have special requirements, so make sure that the model(s) you choose have all the features you are likely to use. Any of the marine models should be fine, but a little research will pay off. I won't cover the details exhaustively, but at a minimum you want a 12-channel model with NMEA capabilities. NMEA allows the GPS to communicate with other electronic devices like your radar and computer. I was a latecomer to electronic charts, but I am now a proselytizing convert.

EPIRB/GPIRB

I carried an EPIRB aboard Topaz, and am glad I never had an occasion to use it. Although it is no guarantee of rescue, an EPIRB can greatly increase the odds. They are expensive, but buying one is like buying insurance, and in the case of an EPIRB you can at least get some of your money back. I bought a used but nearly new unit, used it for five years and got half of my money back by selling it to another cruiser. For less than $100.00 a year I had a lifeline. If you are a single-hander, I cannot say it is a must-have. However, if you have crew or family, it would be irresponsible to not have this added layer of protection aboard.

When choosing an EPIRB, do not even consider a class B model. You want a 406MHz model, and if I were you, I would spring for a GPS-equipped model (GPIRB). As for whether you want a manual or automatically deploying model, it is a toss-up. I treated mine like a personal unit and had it ready and waiting with a lanyard that I could quickly attach to my body. I figured that if I were with the boat, rescuers would find it and me. If I somehow got separated from the boat, I wanted the cavalry to be looking for me, not Topaz. With that in mind, I would seriously consider buying a personal unit as a backup. There were several times when I could have gone over the side, and my friends had similar close calls. Anyone standing watch would feel a little bit better with an EPIRB strapped to his or her waist.

Radar

Radar seems like a luxury limited to bigger boats and bigger budgets. It isn't. Without qualification I can say that except for my GPS, no other item had a bigger role in my successful solo circumnavigation. If I had crew aboard, the radar's importance would have lessened, but not a whole lot. I figure my radar cost me a dollar a day. I would cut back on the Gin and Tonics before I would decide to go offshore without radar.

Like the GPS, radar offers more than you may realize. I used it primarily as a watch stander, and when underway I kept it on 24/7. As soon as I cleared land I would set its zone alarm to go off if it detected any contact. My experience has taught me that the Raytheon was a much more effective watch stander than me, or any other person for that matter. It could spot ships barely visible with binoculars on a clear day and invisible ones when it was stormy. The same is true for spotting land.

The warning I found to be most helpful was not the one that alerted me to land or ships, but the heads-up given for an approaching squall. I cannot count the times when the radar gave me the time to prepare for the brutal winds of fast-moving squall.

The radar also made it possible for me to enter a number of ports in darkness and downpours. It not only did an excellent job of picking up the shoreline, it was also able to spot surf breaks and pesky fishing boats. It is also a great tool for helping confirm position and chart accuracy. By connecting it to a GPS, you can measure distances to objects and via triangulation confirm the boat's position. Once you are in the harbor, it can help you pick your way through the anchored boats and find a place to drop the hook. On especially stormy nights I used it as an anchor watch. Where GPS and depth sounders can sometimes let you know if your anchor is dragging, they cannot tell you if some other yacht is bearing down on you. Radar can.

When selecting radar, buy a good one. My personal opinion is that Raytheon makes the best, with Furuno a close second. The performance of the two brands is similar, but the software on the Raytheon is intuitive and first rate. Don't try to save fifty cents a day by buying a "budget" brand with limited abilities.

I mast mounted my radome on a hydraulically dampened gimbal. I cannot say for certain, but I am convinced that the gimbal contributed greatly to the radar's effectiveness. The radome seemed eerily stable when nothing else aboard was, and if you think about how radar works, stability is very important. A good gimbaled mount is expensive, but I would buy one again.

Tip #1: Experiment with your radar before you head offshore. Just like your boat, radar performs differently under different conditions. In calm conditions it seemed I could "see" container ships that were over the horizon. During a storm I was better limiting its range to 4–6 miles. Generally speaking, the auto-tuning on a quality set will offer the best results, but adjusting ranges and sensitivities can have a huge impact on what the unit will and won't pick up.

Tip #2: I found that I needed to create a doughnut-shaped zone alarm to avoid false alarms due to waves near the boat. If this feature is not available, I would look at other units.

VHF

Of course you will have a VHF. In the U.S., VHF communications are controlled and they rarely get used. Most everywhere else they are a boat's telephone. Cruisers use them all the time for everything. By my estimation they use them too much. I mean, really, for those of you in Marina de la Paz, could you just walk to the next dock instead on getting on the radio every five minutes? I tried to keep my radio off as much as possible, but even I found a hand-held occasionally useful. It is also a good idea to have a hand-held available in the event you have to abandon ship.

Tip #1: Check your antenna wiring before heading offshore. Poor connections and old, corroded wiring are the primary causes of poor radio signal.

Tip # 2: VHF is line-of-sight. The higher the antenna, the longer the range. If your antenna is not at the top of your mast, consider putting it up there.

Depth Sounder

I did a lot of sailing without a depth sounder. In fact, I made it all of the way from Seattle to Ensenada with just a lead line and cautious sailing. I have never been very good at using a conventional depth sounder. I apparently have some sort of spatial difficulty that never really allowed me to learn much from a depth sounder except that I was in trouble. That changed when I hauled in Ensenada and installed an Interphase Probe.

Interphase introduced their line of array-based depth sounders just before I decided to head offshore. Utilizing what is essentially an array of transponders and clever software, they paint a picture of the bottom. Not only does the Probe give the depth of the water under the boat, it shows an image of the terrain in front of the boat. Simply put, these wonderful devices let the boater see where they are going. Finally, a depth sounder even I could use!

Mine was an early model and the software was quite buggy. The auto depth feature and the depth alarm were worthless. Because the viewable distance in front of the boat was directly related to the selected depth range, judicious manual control of the settings was needed to produce the best results. The Probe required quite a bit of practice and settings adjustments to perform up to par. Without this kind of attention, it could be potentially dangerous to rely on the information it provided. I expect and hope theses flaws were improved in later models.

I have heard some claim that the product was gimmicky and not really very useful. Flaws aside, I could not disagree more. In the reef- and coral-head-strewn waters of the South Pacific, every aid to navigation is an asset; the ability to see an underwater obstruction or shoal is priceless. With the radar giving me a picture of the world above the water and the Probe the world below, I had great confidence in my ability to safely navigate just about anywhere. Many times this trusty combo let me enter harbors at night and during periods of low visibility. I will never go offshore with a conventional depth sounder again. Even with its shortcomings, it is a revolutionary product and one I highly recommend.

Not Necessarily Required

Computers

I do all my writing on a computer. I use a digital camera for all of my photos. I have a strong preference for electronic charts, and a computer is one of the best ways to view them. If you don't write or take digital pictures you can get by without a computer, but if you are like me and find computer essential, take two. They are so inexpensive these days and even the best laptops view life aboard as a hazard.

Wind Instruments

A wind indicator is essential, but digital readouts of wind speed, angle, and temperature aren't. If they came with your yacht, great, otherwise save your money. By the time you finish your first ocean crossing you will have more time behind the helm than most sailors accrue in their entire life. You will know what 10, 20, and 40 knots of wind feels and sounds like.

SSB

I confess, in the latter stages of my circumnavigation I oftentimes wished I had a Single Sideband Radio aboard. I covered a lot of lonely miles, and the ability to chat or exchange e-mail would have been wonderful.

Budget allowing, I might opt for an SSB the next time, perhaps not. I expect that technology will soon supplant the SSB and even now satellite phones are a tempting alternative. The total cost of purchasing and installing an SSB would pay for a lot of satellite phone airtime.

If you do opt for an SSB, you will find it handy. Besides ship-to-ship and ship-to-shore communications, you can send and receive e-mail with some add-ons and subscription services. If I consider all the money I spent in Internet cafes, the SSB doesn't look quite so expensive.

If you do not have an SSB, a receiver is a necessity. I had one aboard and it allowed me to listen to weather predictions and the cruiser nets. It will allow you to stay informed and somewhat involved.

Weather FAX and Forecast Services

I am a cynic when it comes to weather prediction, perhaps because I live in the Pacific Northwest where the weather predictions are famously terrible. I often say that if the forecasters predicted rain every day, they would be more accurate than they are now. I feel somewhat the same about the forecasting available to sailors. Every time I used a weather forecast to pick my departure date, I got creamed. I have seen so many cruisers live their lives around weather forecasting and weather faxes, and I think it is mostly a waste of time.

For most of the world, as long as you avoid the cyclone and hurricane seasons, the worst conditions you are likely to encounter are easily handled by a well-founded yacht and crew. On long passages, weather forecasts, assuming they are accurate, can only help with the first part of the trip. I am familiar with the arguments for weather faxes and predictions—chiefly, the ability to sail around fronts and storms—but I think for most of us, these arguments are questionable.

Loran, Etc.

Loran, Lorenz, RDF, VOR, uhhhh... What was that again? I never used the earlier generations of electronic navigation and cannot really say how effective they are. With the advent of GPS, these others have fallen off most sailors' radars. If you can even find them, you can do without them, especially considering they are not now and never have been supported in most of the places you are going.

Gimbaled Radar

Self-Steering

I cannot think of a quicker way to turn adventure into drudgery than sailing without self-steering. A yacht with a large number of crew can pull it off. Even a family of four might manage with regimented shift changes, good luck, and no injuries. For a couple to take turns manning the helm on a passage of any length is asking too much, and if one of them becomes disabled, their prospects become nightmarish. For a solo sailor, it is nearly impossible. Some form of self-steering is required, and I suggest you have two options aboard.

There is no debate about whether self-steering should be used but there are huge debates about which kind is best. They begin with autopilot vs. wind vane, and then progress to which kind of wind vane or autopilot. All considered, the array is vast and confusing. But my position whittles this confusion down pretty quickly. I say you should have both.

Sometimes a wind vane is superior and sometimes only an autopilot will work. Sometimes, one or the other is just easier to manage. When there is little or no wind, a wind vane might as well be a teapot. The same can be said of an autopilot if the conditions are extremely rough with shifting winds. Autopilots are also prone to failure. I have never come across a cruiser whose autopilot did not pack it in at some point. As with every critical piece of equipment aboard, a cruiser should have some form of backup. Sometimes that means carrying spares or the materials needed to effect a repair. In this instance, equipping your yacht with a wind vane and an autopilot offers the benefits of and backup for both.

I sailed with a Monitor wind vane and I used a tiller pilot attached to the Monitor's paddle as my autopilot. Early on, I used the tiller pilot sparingly. Later in my circumnavigation I found myself using it just as much as the wind vane alone. It is simply true that managing an autopilot is easier than a wind vane, and even more so in light wind when running. To the autopilot devotees among my readers: I completely understand, and I would not want to sail without one, either. But, having said that, if you are forced to choose one or the other you will want to take the wind vane.

An autopilot is hot and cold running water, ice cubes, and a fresh water shower. A wind vane is a life raft, EPIRB, and hurricane hole. Most blue water sailors have a love affair with their wind vane. It is hard not to swoon when thinking about the utter brilliance of this remarkably simple invention. When conditions overpower and confuse an autopilot, a wind vane effortlessly steers the boat in a way that is both mesmerizing and magical. During the times when all the crew cares about is staying alive, the wind vane silently and effectively mans the helm. And it does it all without a trickle of electricity. It is not possible to overstate the value of a good wind vane.

If your budget allows, invest in an oversized, high quality, rudder-post-mounted autopilot and a wind vane. This gives you something my setup on Topaz would not—complete redundancy. When I attached the tiller pilot to the wind vane, its functioning relied on both the wind vane and the steering system. If for some reason the wind vane was disabled I would have lost all self-steering capabilities. If a steering cable broke, I would have lost all steering control. A below-deck autopilot is a viable backup to the wind vane and steering system. If you cannot afford it, then do what I did and use a tiller pilot with the wind vane. If you can, take two tiller pilots. Mine lasted the entire circumnavigation, but I had to repair it a few times. But whatever you do, do not leave without a wind vane.

I am a lover of innovation and I eagerly anticipate technological breakthroughs of all kinds. Whatever supposed benefits are offered by the upstarts and one-offs, however, they do not balance the tried and true performance and reliability of a Monitor wind vane. Blue water cruising is a serious business and you and your family should not take on the role of test pilots. I will cover the Monitor's few weak points in the next chapter, but they are niggling when compared to its assets. Please, please, please take my word on this.

The Monitor

Tried and Tested

The first time I saw a Monitor in person was in 1997 aboard New World. I met Lee in Nuku Hiva and one of the first things we did together was remove his Monitor so it could be repaired. His was one of the earlier models that lacked a support tube for the stanchion posts. One of his had cracked and he was forced to apply a Luke anchor shank splint to make it into port. The same kind of cross support Lee added is now standard on all new Monitors. Halfway through my circumnavigation I received an engineering update from Scanmar for a modification intended to reduce watervane shaft breakage.

The Monitor has been around for years, and yet improvements continue to be made. It is this kind of long term and constant improvement that has made the Monitor the preferred wind vane of blue water sailors; that, and its amazing performance. It is also why I recommend it over any other wind vane on the market. Even if someone invents a technologically superior product, it will be years before it will be tested as thoroughly as the Monitor has been.

Purchasing a Monitor

Used Monitors regularly come on the market. They almost always cost exactly half of what a new one does. Deciding to buy used or new can be a toss-up. When you head offshore, you want your wind vane to be in tip-top shape. I installed a new Monitor on Topaz when I left Seattle. I had to replace a number of its rollers and bearings in Africa. I also had to have some touch-up welding done. Ocean sailing is hard on everything. It makes no sense to start your journey with a wind vane that has not been restored to like-new condition.

Unless you buy a used monitor that has been very lightly used, it will need to be rebuilt. It will also need to be inspected for any kind of structural weakening or failure. To save weight, the Monitor is made of relatively thin-walled stainless tube. With repeated strain it has a tendency to crack. Proper installation will eliminate this tendency, but you have no control over how a used wind vane was installed and used before you bought it. You will also have to order custom mounting tubes to fit your yacht as well as a rebuild kit. Add the cost of a couple of airvanes and pendulum line, and the cost difference between used and new shrinks.

Buying used can save you money if you buy judiciously and can do all the repair and restoration work yourself. For about $1000 all told, you can ship your used Monitor to Scanmar and they will professionally restore and rebuild it. That is probably the best option. If money is not a critical issue, buy new. If every dollar counts, start your search for an immaculate Monitor priced right. This search can take time. I intended to buy used, but during my six month search, not a single Monitor came on the market. As soon as I ordered my new one, three used ones came up for sale. Go figure.

Installing the Monitor

Whether you buy new or used, the fine folks at Scanmar will do everything they can to assist you. A unit purchased from them will come with custom mounting tubes and detailed instructions. If you buy used, they provide the same for a nominal fee.

Tremendous forces will be placed on the wind vane and related equipment. It is critical that the installation of the entire system be done properly. It is also important that all the lines, turning blocks, and pulleys be up to the task. I have seen a possibly defective Garhaur turning block come apart in two hours under moderate conditions.

In addition to properly sized and mounted equipment, you must be certain that the wind vane will not move at all under any conditions. Any movement will result in cracks in the tube and eventual failure. The primary causes of movement are loose connections and poorly placed mounting tubes. The connection rigidity can be achieved by making sure that you don't leave out the bolt sleeves that fit inside the tubes. Without them the tube will tend to collapse and you will never get the bolts tight enough.

Proper placement of the mounting tubes is critical. The forces on the wind vane are primarily side-to-side. As the watervane moves back and forth, the force transferred through the pendulum lines will try to loosen the mounting bolts at the base of the stanchion posts. It was my experience that the seizing wire was not strong enough to prevent this. The movement would first break the seizing wire and continue to loosen the bolt until it drops into the sea. In the right conditions, this could happen overnight.

My problem was caused because Topaz's stern is quite narrow and the lower mounting tubes were perpendicular with the stern. The side-to-side force used the tubes like a lever to loosen the bolts. There was no amount of tightening or wire that could stop this. The only solution was for me to weld the mounting tubes to the stanchion posts. If you are able to mount the lower tubes at a 45-degree angle, this will likely eliminate the problem. It is also possible that cross bracing can help. I happen to think that welding the tube in place is a good idea for any boat.

This modification causes no real harm. In fact, it is something I think Scanmar should do as a matter of course. The upper tube mounts are a fixed part of the frame. There is no reason why the bottom could not be as well. The current design makes mounting a little easier but I do not believe it is worth the potential price. A few extra hours on the dock beats hanging over the stern while underway. It isn't fun.

Spares

The Monitor is extremely well-made. In fact, it is a work of art. It is strong and reliable but it is subject to wear and tear like any other mechanical device. If you only plan to sail a few miles and not far from civilization, you might not need any spare parts. If, however, you plan to cross an ocean or sail for any extended period of time, there are a number of spare parts you really must take with you.

Spectra Pendulum Line

The line provided by Scanmar is specially made with linear, not woven, Spectra fibers. The pendulum lines operate under extreme loads that will quickly stretch conventional "low stretch" line. When the time came to replace my pendulum lines, I was in Tahiti. I was forced to choose braided Spectra and I battled the stretching for many miles. Even so, I was lucky to find any kind of low stretch line. Make sure you have enough spare pendulum line to effect a complete replacement.

You can get extra miles from your pendulum lines by having them a couple feet longer than necessary. This will allow you to repeatedly shift the line so as to move the sections that get run over the blocks into less demanding areas.

Safety Tubes

I say tubes because I believe you should have several aboard. I went through half a dozen during my journey, and it was a relief to know that I always had a spare tucked below. There is no way to predict how many you will need or how often they will break. Some cruisers never break one and others go through many. I suggest having at least two spares.

Airvanes

I never had one break, but I did have a couple that warped. I also had one go over the side (a lanyard will help prevent this). Partway through my circumnavigation, Scanmar came out with a light airvane. Through the grapevine I heard that offshore racers were using the paddle in winds up to 50 knots. I bought one and it became my primary. I would say that it would be a good start to have two of each kind aboard. That gives you a total of three spares.

I have heard of some sailors making their own, but this is harder than it looks. Scanmar has a section in their manual that will help if you must make one. Their manual is one of the best I have seen for any kind of equipment. Read it a couple of times before you head offshore.

Rebuild Kit

By the time my fellow cruisers made it from Mexico to Africa, it was time to do a full or partial rebuild of the Monitor. While it sounds dramatic, a rebuild is really just a replacement of sheaves, bushings and bearings. This is not a difficult task. At a minimum you might have to change the sheaves. If you travel across a couple of oceans, you will need to do more. Having a complete rebuild kit aboard will allow you to maintain your Monitor as needed and it will provide a nice pile of spare parts. Scanmar sells a Cruising Parts Kit which is a good starting point, but the last time I checked, it did not include all of the bearings and sheaves needed for a rebuild. A conversation with them will allow you to augment the Cruising Kit to give you everything you will need.

Parts I Had to Replace

I cover most of this list in the other sections, but it provides a quick look at the spares you will want to stock, starting from the top.

Airvane: They can break, warp, and go over the side.

Pendulum Line: It is hard to find replacement line so take enough to replace all your line.

Pendulum Line Sheaves: These are unlikely to wear out completely but they will wear enough to warrant replacement.

Stanchion Post Mounting Bolt: If you do not weld this connection, it is possible that you will lose one of these bolts along the way. These have seizing wire holes in their heads so grab a couple extra just in case; seizing wire, too.

Hinge Pin and Retaining Ring: My pin tended to rotate, which wore through a couple of retaining rings. This resulted in some lost pins. In a pinch, a bolt will get you through, but I would carry a couple of spares. I found that a nylon washer between the retaining ring and hinge body prevented the wear on the retaining ring.

Hinge Spring: Mine eventually broke. Without it the hinge won't stay closed. The loss of this tiny part makes it impossible to keep the watervane in the water.

Safety Tube: These are intended to break in the event of a collision. Mine tended to break due to wear and flexing. Take a couple of extras.

Wheel Adapter Connection: The spokes on Topaz's wheel are quite thin. The hose clamps continually broke because the base of the clamp was wider than the spoke, causing part of the clamp to be bent at a right angle. Adding hard rubber bushings between the clamps and the spokes eliminated this problem. It also allowed the use of a larger clamp.

Suggested Modifications

Watervane Tube: I found that over time, cracks developed in the watervane mounting tube. This was caused by the constant motion and flexibility of the tube. By welding stainless washers over the holes, you will eliminate the problem.

Delrin Adustment Pulley

It was not long before the base of my adjustment pulley started to crack. The pressure of the set screw accentuated this and soon the pulley was slipping. My solution was to reinforce the shoulder of the pulley with a hose clamp. I then drilled a recess into the pilot shaft so the set screw could not slip.

Because of the mounting difficulties, my Monitor endured more abuse than most. Other cruisers I know experienced none of these issues and other cruisers had issues I did not. These comments are in no way intended to impugn the quality of the Monitor. Rather, I am noting things that are important to, well, monitor.

Modifications to the Monitor

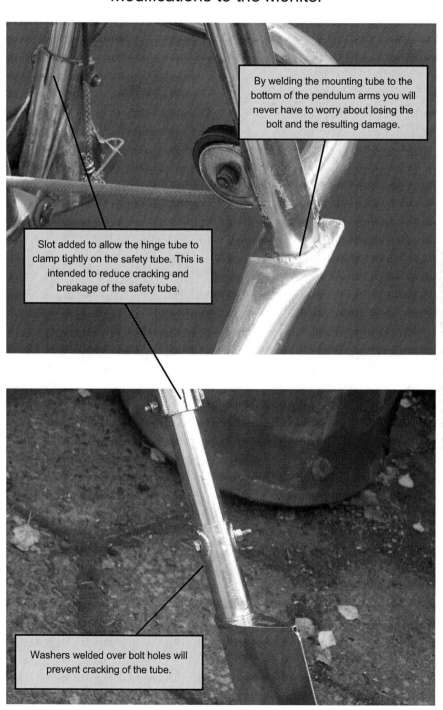

By welding the mounting tube to the bottom of the pendulum arms you will never have to worry about losing the bolt and the resulting damage.

Slot added to allow the hinge tube to clamp tightly on the safety tube. This is intended to reduce cracking and breakage of the safety tube.

Washers welded over bolt holes will prevent cracking of the tube.

Yacht Tender

Yacht Tender

On this subject the advice is as confusing as on any other. Some cruisers swear by their big, aluminum, custom-made tender. Others spring for very expensive fiberglass rowing–sailing dinghies. After a time you will get the sense that an inflatable is the last resort if space is an issue. I say, "Rubbish!" In every case, a well-made inflatable dinghy is the best option.

An inflatable dinghy offers the most stable platform and comfortable ride of all of the dinghy options. This is a big deal. When loading or unloading provisions, snorkeling, or just getting in or out of the dinghy, the inflated tubes guarantee you will never capsize. As for durability, a well-made inflatable of hypalon material will endure more than you are likely to inflict on it. During the research required to write my books and daily use over a five-year circumnavigation, I hit hundreds of beaches, picked my way through coral reefs, and played tug to dozens of boats in need. My inflatable bore many scars but never suffered a puncture.

All inflatables are not the same, however. Most live up to the reputation of being hard to row, very wet underway and plagued with maintenance concerns. The easiest way to avoid all of the above is to buy either a Caribe or A/B. I understand that the same factory makes both, but the trim packages vary. These dinghies are made of very thick hypalon material. The tube diameters are the largest on the market and these dinghies are shaped for improved stability and less spray when underway. The non-RIB models come with an inflatable keel that is prominent enough to make rowing easy and the tracking razor sharp. I think Avon makes the next best thing, but when sitting next to a Caribe or A/B the Avon looks somewhat anemic.

Do not let cost dictate your dinghy decisions. In every case, the difference between the cheapest and most expensive option is not enough to make scrimping worthwhile. Your dinghy is your car. It is your delivery truck, your ambulance, and your recreational vehicle. For some, myself included, it can double as a life raft option. Buy the best dinghy available and the biggest you feel you can physically manage. The difference in cost between the 9-foot and 11-foot models is nothing compared to the bigger model's greater capability. I was alone and had the 11-foot model. I would never settle for an 8-foot or 9-foot dinghy except as a backup. They are just too small.

Speaking of backups, I was a crewmember when I experienced my first blue water passage. My first tropical anchorage was the magnificent Taiohae, Nuku Hiva. One night we went to bed with our inflatable tied to the rail and the following morning it was gone. Luckily, my skipper carried a spare hard dinghy. Without it we would have been dependent upon other cruisers until we arrived in Papeete.

Tahiti is the last place in the world where one would want to buy anything, let alone a dinghy. But as expensive as Tahiti is, at least you can buy dinghies there. In most places in the world, you can't. When I set sail on my own boat, I took the lesson to heart and brought along a fiberglass Sabot as a spare.

I was glad I did. There were times when I needed to get a dinghy in the water in minutes, and getting a large inflatable ready to launch takes time. There were other occasions when I was only going to be in an anchorage overnight and I was willing to make do with the hard dink. In the last, and worst case, my inflatable was stolen in Venezuela and the backup dinghy was promoted.

If I were to do it again, I would carry a spare but I would make it a smaller inflatable. While your primary dinghy needs to be as big and as new as possible, your backup can be smaller with some miles on it. The spare should be small enough to fit on the deck in "ready to use" condition. That means fully inflated with the oars inside. You will not need to worry about sun damage if you have chosen a high quality dinghy made of hypalon.

Sailing Rig?

If you are a real lover of dinghy sailing then you may want your backup to be a hard dink with a sailing rig. Truth be told, in all my years of sailing, I can count on one hand the number of times I saw sailors putting around the bay in a sailing dinghy. Just about all of us got our fill of sailing on the passages and changing anchorages. Keep that in mind as you relegate precious storage space to sails, rudder, dagger board and mast. I left with a sailing rig but eventually let some other cruiser pay for the privilege of storing it on their boat.

Accessories

You will need at least one set of oars. Having a backup set is not a bad idea. When my dinghy was stolen in Venezuela, I searched in vain for a pair of oars to replace the set that was in the inflatable. Until I found a cruiser willing to part with their spare set I had to flounder around the bay with what was literally a plastic toy. My original set was aluminum shafted with a plastic blade. If you hate sanding and varnishing as much as I do, avoid wood oars.

A strong and reliable tether is critical. Repeated use and bad weather will take a toll on the dinghy painter. I highly recommend setting up a harness system (see illustration) and using a stainless carabineer as a fastener. Doing so not only saves the time and trouble of tying and untying, it also eliminates the chance of the dinghy getting free. I have seen many dinghies liberated from the mother ship due to chafe, badly tied knots and too many Margaritas. Topaz has a perforated aluminum rail which was a perfect fastening point for the carabineer. If your yacht lacks such a rail, permanent and secure connection points can easily be added. There are more than enough opportunities aboard for knot tying exercises. Eliminating this one adds peace of mind and more than a little convenience.

Wheels

If you opt for a large dinghy and are alone, then wheels don't help. The wheels mounted on the stern require you to pick up the entire length of the dinghy. It is easier to drag the dinghy than it is to lift and pull. If you have two people, the wheels help but are unnecessary. By the time I was a year out, all of us seemed to be carrying around a broken set of wheels. I would say that until someone invents a sturdy set of wheels that somehow supports the dinghy's weight, I would save my money. Except in Darwin, Australia, where the tide leaves a quarter mile of beach to traverse, I did not need any wheels.

The Outboard

You are going to want an outboard big enough to easily put your dinghy on plane with the average number of people you will carry on a daily basis. My 11-foot dinghy needed a 10hp motor to get on plane with four average sized people in it. To do this someone needed to move forward to put weight in the bow to get the plane started. If I was planning on having four people all of the time I would have moved up to a 15hp. Many people settle for tiny outboards that do little more than relieve them of rowing duties. Adding a correctly sized outboard to a large dinghy will open up a whole world of recreational opportunities. It will also allow you to use your tender as a tug should your yacht or others' need help.

I used a 2-stroke Johnson, which turned out to be a perfect choice. These outboards are used all around the world so spare parts are easy to come by. Anyone who knows me will attest to the fact that my outboard was brutally treated. I never once flushed it with fresh water. I ran it at top speed everywhere I went and I ran it into sand and coral bottoms almost daily. It was a few years old but only slightly used when I bought it. In the four years that I used it, I had to replace the cooling water impeller, the start rope and the start spring. This is an excellent testament to its reliability.

Which Brand?

I do not have vast experience with different kinds of outboards. I have only used Hondas and Johnsons, both excellent machines. My general feeling is that if you stick with a reputable brand, you will have good luck. Although 2-stroke models are getting harder and harder to find, they are the best choice. They are lighter and require less maintenance than their 4-stroke counterparts. Oil for mixing and spare parts are universal as the fishermen of the world are great users of outboard motors. There are very few ports where outboards and a way to get parts are not available.

Tender Details

The harness shown below provides the most secure and stable way to secure your inflatable. The stock D-ring attachment points cannot endure years of heavy use. Even though is is heavily discouraged by the "experts," most of us tow our dinghies around and between anchorages. I have even, admittedly foolishly, towed mine on overnight passages. The system below endured a 140 mile beat in a horrific storm.

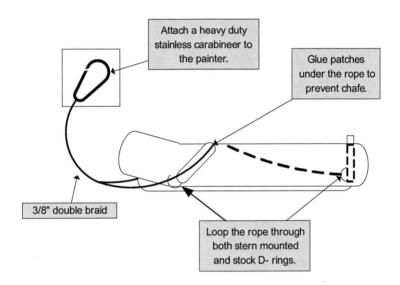

Attach a heavy duty stainless carabineer to the painter.

Glue patches under the rope to prevent chafe.

3/8" double braid

Loop the rope through both stern mounted and stock D- rings.

Photo Estelle Shives

Provisioning

If you are going to be traveling for years, it only makes sense that you will eventually need to rely on whatever goods are available in the countries you visit. The concern that you need to carry enough of any specific item to last you forever is both unfounded and unrealistic. The best way to approach provisioning is to stock up on whatever you can in every port and adapt as you move around the world.

In most books about cruising, authors make it seem as though you need to plan like you are heading out on a mission to Mars where it is not even certain that you will encounter water. The truth is that wherever people are living, there is an abundance of good food to be had. No, you won't find French Brie in Tonga but you will find plenty of other great things to eat. Fresh vegetables are everywhere. Fish and fowl are everywhere. All of the ingredients for bread can be found everywhere. In fact, because the places you will likely visit have limited access to refrigeration, they have many things that we do not that are perfect for cruising. Canned butter and whole milk powder are just two examples.

I strongly believe that food is one of life's greatest pleasures. It is true on land as well as aboard. I found that my provisioning worked best when I did not put any limits on my food budget. Before leaving each port I would visit the supermarkets or shops and buy anything and everything I needed and that appealed to me. I focused especially on long life items like canned or dry goods. I felt no need to deny myself anything, and found that the splurges became important morale-boosters during difficult times. I promise you that during a passage you will never feel guilt for having a pricey delicacy aboard.

The only area I went overboard on was jelly and jam. I never have eaten much jelly but for some odd reason I found myself unable to resist buying half a dozen jars whenever I came across them. When I finished my circumnavigation I probably had 20 jars stashed around the boat. I never did eat them.

Most dry and canned items have a shelf life measured in years. My jelly fixation notwithstanding, there is no real harm in having 20 cans of beans or an extra five pounds of flour. In time, it will all get eaten. These long life items are indeed staples. They will sometimes supplement the fresh foods you will find and other times make up the entire meal. Having both quantity and a variety of canned and dry goods will ensure that you never go without, especially when fresh food is limited or unavailable.

If you spend most of your time near population centers, having fresh food aboard is easy. This is not so during long passages or if you venture away from primary ports. Nothing fresh lasts very long in the tropics. Except for potatoes, onions, cabbage and squash, your vegetables will do well to last a week. Some cruisers utilize refrigeration to extend their life but it takes an awfully big refrigerator to make much of a difference. If you are at all adventurous, there will be many times when dry and canned is all you have to choose from.

The real keys to provisioning are creativity, an open mind, and the willingness to experiment and incorporate the local foods into your diet. If you do this, your provisioning will be interesting and easy. Along the way you will have the opportunity to fall in love with Poisson Cru, taro, and even dishes like canned corned beef in coconut milk. There will be times when you cannot find things you long for and even moments when a 7-11 seems like a shopping extravaganza. Mostly, however, you will come to enjoy the challenge and discovery that provisioning in foreign lands offers.

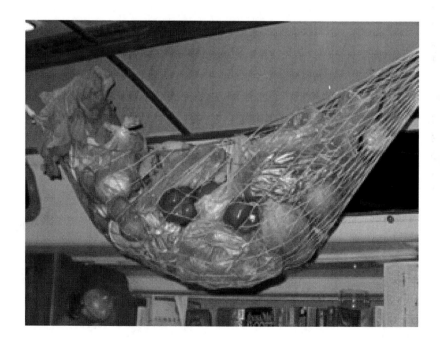

Navigation

Electronic Charts, GPS, and Cruising Guides

I know this is heresy but I would not spend thousands of dollars on paper charts. Instead, I would buy cruising guides, a couple GPS's, and a few large-scale area charts. Then I would scrounge around until I found a copy of the latest CMAP beta CD that practically every long range cruiser seems to have aboard. This disk contains electronic charts for the entire world. They are remarkably accurate and compatible with NMEA devices.

Honey! Where's the Sextant?

Conventional wisdom dictates that a cruiser must have a complete set of paper charts and a sextant aboard their yacht. The fact is most cruisers sail with neither a sextant nor a complete set of charts. Many who have a sextant cannot use it and those who can, treat it as entertainment more than a tool. The dogmatic scream *travesty* but I find it hard to get too exercised over the matter.

The truth is that GPS and electronic charts have withered the traditional navigational skills of most cruisers. I am one of them. At some level it is defensible. I challenge you not to fall in love with a system that shows your current location with pinpoint accuracy. It is uncanny to look at the screen and have whirling satellites and software show you the exact slip your yacht is moored in.

Traditional navigation simply cannot compete with the accuracy of today's electronics. Even the old school purists have to admit that a sextant is not much use when trying to navigate through the Tuamotus. GPS and electronic charts are remarkably accurate, and unless there is some kind of system failure, very reliable.

I am not suggesting that you sail without paper charts or a sextant. I happen to believe that the more spares, the more backups and the more aids to navigation the better. At some point, however, space and money call for prioritization. I believe a judicious use of key paper charts, electronic charts, GPS, and cruising guides will allow you to safely navigate the waters of the world. I and almost every other cruiser have done so.

Disclaimer

I have re-written this section many times and given the chance, I might do it again. Anytime one gives advice from any position of authority one feels a certain amount of responsibility. As with all the other advice I give in this book, it is up to you to decide what you feel is appropriate and safe.

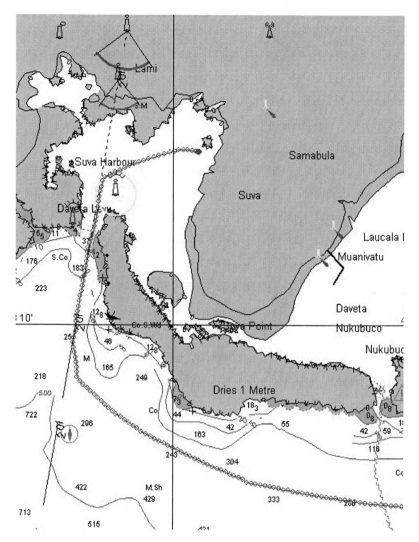

This is a screen capture of my tracked route into Suva Harbor, Fiji. Utilizing a combination of GPS, electronic charts, depth sounder and Radar I was able to safely and accurately enter the harbor during zero visibility. I used radar ranging and triangulation to verify electronic chart accuracy. The radar picked up surf breaks as well as land and light towers.

Emergency Preparedness

You Are All Alone

By its nature, blue water cruising demands self-reliance. There will be times when the only aid available is whatever happens to be aboard your yacht. Whether you need a doctor, mechanic, or rescuer, your task is to meet those needs yourself. Below I list what I think is most important, but do not limit your considerations to what I have written here. There are infinite scenarios that can put you and your crew at risk. It is impossible to plan for every situation, but it is possible to plan for the most dire.

Imagine...

As important as supplies and training is the contemplation of emergency scenarios. Reading books like Steven Callahan's "Adrift" will help focus the mind on what is most important. Read a few books, then sit in the cockpit and fantasize. Contemplate an entire passage and what you would do in response to every disaster you can imagine. Think about what you would do if you hit the rocks leaving the harbor and your yacht started to sink. Imagine you are a thousand miles from anywhere when the boom slices open your head, you lose a finger, or a fall fractures your arm. What about food poisoning or appendicitis? What will you do if the rudder falls off or the mast goes over the side? At what point will you abandon ship and how will you do so? It might seem gruesome, but visualizing potential disasters will help you prepare for and perhaps avoid them.

Abandoning Ship

For most sailors, this is the Big Kahuna. It is hard to imagine anything worse than bobbing around the sea in a life raft. As a solo sailor, I always figured falling overboard was even worse, as I had no hope of anyone turning the boat around to come pick me up. In either case, contemplating the loss of one's yacht is horrifying. We have all heard the abandoned yacht stories where the yacht survives but the crew didn't. With that in mind, spend a lot of time figuring out exactly what your abandon ship threshold is. I love the quote, "One should step up to get into the life raft." The point being that you should not abandon your yacht until its rail is lower in the water than the life raft.

I cannot think of any reason to get off of a yacht that is not either ablaze or going under to get into a small rubber raft. Many people have done just that and I do not really understand why. I suppose the name "life raft" inspires some sense of comfort or refuge. Perhaps they should be named "chance rafts" because that is all they offer, a chance. In every way, your yacht is the best place to stay and I would not get into the raft until the rail is going under. No matter how rough it seems on the boat, the life raft will be no more comfortable. The yacht is the repository for all of your supplies including food, water, clothing and navigational aids. Until it sinks, it is the true life raft.

Life Raft or Dinghy?

This is not a ridiculous question. Reasonable people can and do disagree about whether a dinghy can serve as a life raft. I happen to be one of those who believe a dinghy can be a superior choice.

In the interest of full disclosure I must admit that I sailed without a life raft. My abandon ship plan was never tested and I admit that it was not very tightly scripted. It involved my abandon ship bags, which consisted of two, watertight five-gallon buckets full of supplies, a hard dinghy and my inflatable. I also had an immersion suit at the ready.

If I had time, I planned to deploy the hard dink, inflate the other and load up both with as many supplies as I could. This included the watermaker. Because I was alone and a pretty hardy soul, I figured that if I needed to, I could lash everything together, toss it over the side, flounder around in the sea and sort it out later. Not very scientific but I felt confident I would find a way to survive.

It is my proactive nature that causes me to lean toward choosing an inflatable dinghy over a life raft. I want the opportunity to contribute to my survival and rescue. The ability to row and sail a dinghy could make a huge difference. I cannot imagine the trauma of drifting past land in a life raft and being unable to point it toward shore. I am also quite pessimistic about the reliability and durability of life rafts. Perhaps I have read too many stories, but it seems to me that a good number of them fail to work, blow away before one can enter, or leak like a sieve. One thing I knew for certain, my inflatable wasn't going to leak. It was made out of top-quality hypalon and received daily inspections.

I am not going to prescribe which choice is best for you. What I would suggest is exploring all the options, including letting your tender serve double duty. With the proper preparations, I believe that an inflatable can provide a superior emergency platform as well as save you thousands of dollars and precious deck space.

What to Take with You

As I mentioned above, my abandon ship bag was really a pair of five-gallon buckets. I had them connected to each other with a tether that could be quickly attached to my dinghy. I made sure the setup was secure by tossing both buckets over the side while under full sail. I wanted to be sure that they would stay together and remain intact. They did.

Even if you choose a life raft and have it packed with survival gear, there is no reason why you should not supplement your emergency stores in a similar way. If your emergency gear is packed in a container that floats, it is possible to take much more than would normally fit in a raft or a dinghy.

Just because you carry an EPIRB, do not expect anything close to an immediate rescue. Depending on where you are when your yacht goes down, it may take days for help to arrive. If really bad things happen, like your EPIRB fails or you lose it in the confusion, you might really be on your own. Hope for the best but expect the worst.

Again, take some time and imagine yourself stranded for a week or three. Think about all the things you will need and hope to have with you. There is no real limit to the number of safety products available to cruisers, and visualizing your time adrift will help you sift through them. Unfortunately, it is impossible and impractical to prepare for every eventuality. Even if one could, it would require another boat just to haul the necessary supplies. At some point, your choices will be limited by space and money, and like every skipper and crew, you will need to determine which items are priority.

Where There Is No Doctor

This is not only the title of the must-have book by David Werner, it is where you will find yourself much of the time. It might seem too obvious to state, but someone aboard must be conversant in first aid. There should also be a well-stocked first aid and medical kit aboard. There are a number of books and references available that can help you be prepared, but do start with David Werner's fine book.

You can expect to have to deal with periodic cuts, burns and coral induced infections. Every time I had to repair something it seemed to require a blood sacrifice. A high tolerance of pain is a beneficial attribute for a cruiser. Even so, having some strong pain killers are a nice addition to the topical antibiotics and bandages.

Oral antibiotics are a must-have. While it is true that they are overused they are also a medical miracle that just may save your life. During one of my passages I became convinced that I was suffering the onset of appendicitis. Large doses of antibiotics can stave off appendicitis and I started eating Cipro like candy. I don't know if it did any good but I got better.

In all cases follow the Boy Scout motto and *Be Prepared*.

Where in the World?

Where In The World?

I am about to offer somewhat unfair advice. My solo circumnavigation is the toughest and most rewarding thing I have ever done and it is undoubtedly my greatest accomplishment. It *has* both changed and defined me. Despite this, I would not recommend it as a goal unless completing a circumnavigation is at the top of your life-goal list.

The truth is that the vast majority of cruisers who start out with a circumnavigation in mind simply never make it. Of the hundreds of yachts that stream through the Caribbean and South Pacific every year, dozens or fewer reach the Indian Ocean. This is not due to a lack of ability; it is a lack of will and desire. And the cruisers are not to blame. I fault what I call the Jimmy Buffett Effect.

The island life most cruisers discover is so wonderfully rich and easy that leaving it behind becomes more and more difficult. Most every cruiser ends up spending more time than they planned in either the Caribbean or the Pacific. When the time comes to move on, the long ocean passages become less and less appealing. A cheeseburger in paradise trumps a mid-ocean gale every time. This brings us to...

The Great Wall of Australia

By the time most cruisers reach Tonga or Fiji, they will start saying unthinkable things like, "Oh, another island." Yes, one perfect tropical island does start to look like the hundreds you have already seen. After years of too much fun and more than a few bad storms, the Earth's geography offers a dose of reality. The charts are clear. It is a long hard journey from Australia back to the U.S. Even getting to the Med is no easy task and it is made less so by the Middle East turmoil and the pirates that ply the waters around Yemen. Very, very few yachts continue past Australia.

Where Would I Go?

When you are contemplating travel, the options are practically endless. Most places can be reached by plane or vehicle, and others cannot. In my opinion, cruising is best reserved for visiting those places where only a yacht can take you and where having a yacht significantly improves the experience.

Every place seems more interesting when you arrive by yacht. Even lake sailors know this to be true. Having said that, if I lived in Hawaii and wanted to visit Los Angeles, sailing there would not be worth the trouble. It makes a lot more sense to fly. In areas like the South Pacific, the Caribbean, or even the Med, the cruising grounds are so spectacular that yacht travel is well worth the effort. In some island nations it is the only possible way to go.

With that in mind, I would consider how long you want to be gone and plan your trip to maximize the benefits of traveling by yacht. I have found that people who visit the Caribbean first really love it. Cruisers that visit the Pacific first tend to like the Caribbean less. If you like a higher concentration of cruisers without getting too far away from civilization, then the Caribbean is for you. If you don't mind longer passages, less civilization, and fewer cruisers then head to the Pacific. Of course, you can always do both.

Unless you are planning a circumnavigation, where you go will likely depend on where you live now. At some point you will either want to get your yacht back home or sell it overseas. It does not seem to matter where you start your sailing adventure, the winds and seas make it much more difficult to return home than it was to leave. Part of this effect is emotional. Most cruisers tend to get their fill after a time, which is something to keep in mind as you plan your trip.

If I were to do it all over again and planned a journey of three to five years, I would spend most of it in the Pacific. I would plan my itinerary so that the end of my journey would have me circling through Asia and back across the Pacific to my home in Seattle.

This kind of plan allows for a trip as short as one year and as long as one wants. There are thousands of islands, and the ability to utilize the North and South Pacific to avoid cyclones and hurricanes means you never have to stop sailing. For the Caribbean and Med sailors, this is more difficult to accomplish, although the trip home is decidedly easier.

Wherever you decide to go, keep in mind the reality that you might decide to stop cruising sooner than you originally intend. If you decide that you want to return to the United States, this decision is much better made in Fiji than Cocos Keeling.

Is It All Worth It?

Is It All Worth It?

The short answer is yes. Cruising aboard a yacht is unquestionably one of the greatest experiences. It has everything; travel, adventure, risk and a social life richer than any you will likely find ashore. It is an experience that is everything you can imagine and more. Sometimes, it is less. Cruising will change you, and it just may define you. So yes, it is worth it, every bit of it.

It is not an unqualified yes, however. It is only worth it if you actually do it. The sad truth is that most want-to-be-cruisers never leave the dock. Of those who do, most never cross an ocean. For many, life, fear, and finances stop the dream cold. No matter how frugal you are or how much you are willing to sacrifice, cruising is expensive. There are few things sadder than seeing a for-sale sign posted on someone's failed dream.

Dollars and Sense

Right now is the time to be brutally honest with yourself. Do you really have what it takes to cut the ties, endure potentially terrifying seas, and live for at least three years aboard your yacht? If you are uncertain, I suggest you consider other alternatives. There is just no way around it. Even if you can get most of the cost of the boat back by selling her when you return, it is still a costly endeavor.

No matter how you do it, getting started is going to take tens of thousands of dollars. A quick visit to any yacht brokerage or online listing will show you what I mean. On top of the cost of the boat is all the equipment it will need to be cruise-ready. Ask any cruiser and they will tell you that there are no yachts on the market that are ready to go. They all need something, and everything made for oceangoing yachts is expensive. In addition to the capital expense, you will have cost of living, fuel and maintenance, port fees, and other incidentals. Depending on your lifestyle, this will run somewhere between $1000 and $3000 per month. I know it can be done for less, but a tighter budget will cost you some fun.

The Bare Minimum

If you want to cross an ocean, about the least expensive option I would consider is something like a Cal 35. With luck, you can find one for about $25,000. Of course, it will not be ready to take cruising. Unless you get really lucky, expect to spend as much on prep as you did for the boat. This option pretty much sets my lower limit of what a cruise-ready yacht will cost. Also keep in mind that you will probably not get your preparation money back.

It is pretty simple math; fifty thousand for the boat, ten thousand a year to live for a minimum of three years. It adds up fast, but I would not want to do it for less. We cruisers regularly joke that we could have flown around the world, stayed in fine hotels and eaten in fancy restaurants for less than what it costs to go cruising. It is not really a joke.

With so much time and money at stake, I strongly suggest that you volunteer as crew aboard a cruising yacht, preferably on an ocean passage. It is very easy to like Margaritas and sunsets in a beautiful anchorage, but a week underway is a whole different thing. You may find that you love it all, or you may find that the pleasure is not worth the pain. Or, like most, you will decide that you are willing to endure the passages to enjoy the anchorages.

You can be absolutely certain, however, that no matter where you end up your exposure to the cruising lifestyle will be a highlight of your life. Even if you make a passage as crew and decide you really don't like it, you will have done something incredibly memorable and enlightening.

To quote my good friend and experienced cruiser, Cary Derringer, "Just do it."